CROSS STITCH
Countryside Collection

David and Charles

A DAVID & CHARLES BOOK
Copyright © David & Charles Limited 2008

David & Charles is an F+W Publications Inc. company
4700 East Galbraith Road
Cincinnati, OH 45236

First published in the UK in 2008

Text and designs copyright © Claire Crompton, Caroline Palmer,
Lesley Teare and Carol Thornton 2008
Photography, illustrations and layout copyright © David & Charles 2008

A catalogue record for this book is available from the British Library.

ISBN-13: 978-0-7153-2822-4 hardback
ISBN-10: 0-7153-2822-0 hardback

Printed in China by SNP Leefung Pte Ltd
for David & Charles
Brunel House   Newton Abbot   Devon

Senior Commissioning Editor: Cheryl Brown
Desk Editor: Bethany Dymond
Project Editor and Chart Preparation: Lin Clements
Senior Designer: Charly Bailey
Designer: Mia Farrant
Production Controller: Ros Napper

Visit our website at www.davidandcharles.co.uk

David & Charles books are available from all good bookshops; alternatively
you can contact our Orderline on 0870 9908222 or write to us at FREEPOST
EX2 110, D&C Direct, Newton Abbot, TQ12 4ZZ (no stamp required UK only);
US customers call 800-289-0963 and Canadian customers call 800-840-5220.

CONTENTS

INTO THE COUNTRYSIDE. . .

*T*his beautiful collection of evocative cross stitch designs is an unashamedly nostalgic view of the British countryside from years gone by, with idyllic scenes many of us remember fondly from our childhood.

More and more we come to cherish our countryside, guarding it with passion, and sometimes pitchforks, and affectionately capturing the changing faces of our glorious heritage through literature, art, crafts and, of course, our memories. Whether we are city born and bred or hailing from rural parts of the country, this lovely collection of cross stitch designs will bring back memories of how the countryside used to be. These original designs remind us of that simpler, quieter place, where we lived closely in touch with the land and the changing seasons; where joy was found in simple pleasures – a walk through a dappled bluebell wood, watching fields of golden wheat being gathered in, picking rosy apples from the orchard. . .

But we can still catch glimpses of the way the countryside used to be, and in those magical moments we are transported back in time to a rose-tinted age. This atmospheric collection of cross stitch pictures will help you travel back along those primrose paths.

Designed by Claire Crompton

IN THE ORCHARD

A century ago fruit orchards were a common sight, invaluable to families for the fruits essential for pies, jams and preserves and for bringing welcome zest to the table. Apple, pear, plum, damson, cherry and quince were common, plus many soft fruits. Most gardens boasted at least one apple tree, hung in autumn with apples rarely heard of today, such as Nutmeg Pippin, Sops in Wine, Cornish Gilliflower and Greensleeves.

Many of the Shires of England dedicated whole orchards to making cider, that potent drink created from fermented apples. Cider and ale were drunk in quantity on dusty harvest days and mulled to be sipped hot on freezing winter nights. Ripe apples were gathered and laid in the warm September sun to mellow and develop their flavour. They were then ground in stone-wheeled cider mills, worked by sturdy horses. Cider apples had wonderfully descriptive names, such as Fair Maid of Devon, Strawberry Norman and Slack-ma-girdle.

The apple varieties may have diminished but it's still possible to enjoy the sight of orchards laden with juicy fruits and this lovely, tranquil scene reminds us of the beauty that is still all around us.

> "AN APPLE PIE
> WITHOUT SOME CHEESE
> IS LIKE A KISS
> WITHOUT A SQUEEZE."

In this atmospheric design, tart red apples on the bough shine through a canopy of leaves, while a flock of geese treat themselves to the early windfalls that litter the ground. The scene is shown here framed as a picture but it would also make a beautiful cushion.

Apple Orchard Picture

This orchard scene has a lovely mellow feel, with areas of half cross stitch in the sky and background adding to the hazy atmosphere. It could be worked over two threads of a 28-count linen. You could border the design with fabric and create a lovely wall hanging.

STITCH COUNT
149h x 198w

DESIGN SIZE
27.2 x 36cm (10¾ x 14in)

YOU WILL NEED
✧ 42 x 51cm (16½ x 20in)
   cream 14-count Aida
✧ Tapestry needle size 24
✧ DMC stranded cotton (floss)
   as listed in the chart key
✧ Suitable picture frame

> **"** APPLES WATERED
> BY ST SWITHIN'S
> TEARS ARE THE
> MOST LUSCIOUS. **"**

1 Prepare your fabric for work (see page 96). Find and mark the centre of the fabric and the centre of the chart on pages 14–17. For your own use you could photocopy the chart parts and tape them together. Note: some colours use more than one skein – see chart key for details. Mount fabric in an embroidery frame if you wish.

2 Start stitching from the centre of the chart working outwards over one block of Aida (or two threads of linen). Use two strands of stranded cotton for cross stitches and one for backstitches. The backstitches use a 'sketchy' style, which doesn't always follow the cross stitch exactly. For tweeded cross stitches (where two colours are mixed together), use one strand of each colour listed in the key. For areas of half cross stitch, use two strands for the sky and one strand for the ground.

3 Once all the stitching is complete, frame the design as a picture (see page 100) or make up in some other way of your choice.

'A sunny afternoon, with blanket spread,

Beneath some apple trees, with ample shade,

We'd sit with tray of tea and gingerbread,

Scones with jam, and these were all homemade.'

(from 'The Apple Orchard' by Ernestine Northover)

Apple and Mint Jelly

This is a traditional way of preserving mint and is useful for
using up windfallen apples.

✧ Put 1kg (2lbs) of unpeeled, chopped cooking apples into a pan with
150ml (¼ pint) of white wine vinegar and 300ml (½ pint) of water. Boil
and then simmer for an hour until the fruit is pulp. Strain the
fruit over a bowl overnight through a muslin bag.
✧ Put the juice into a pan with 330g (12oz) sugar and heat until
the sugar has dissolved. Boil until it reaches setting point.
✧ Finely chop 50g (2oz) of mint leaves and stir into the liquid.
Leave for ten minutes, stir and then pour into a warm jar.
Allow to cool before adding a lid.

Baking Day Collection

If all the juicy apples in the orchard picture have set your mouth watering, then why not make the handy collection shown here to use in your kitchen? The jar band could also be used on a bottle of apple wine or cider, adjusting the size to fit. Instead of attaching a patch to a pot holder, the design could be used on a ready-made apron.

Autumn Jar Band

Stitch count
38h x 38w

Design size
7 x 7cm (2¾ x 2¾in)

You will need
- ✧ 13 x 13cm (4¾ x 4¾in) cream 14-count Aida
- ✧ Tapestry needle size 24
- ✧ DMC stranded cotton (floss) as listed in the chart key
- ✧ Gingham or patterned fabric for band and lid cover
- ✧ Jam jar with straight sides

1 Stitch the design from page 13 on the Aida fabric using two strands of stranded cotton for cross stitch and French knots.

2 Make up the jar band as follows. Trim the embroidery 2cm (¾in) beyond the widest measurements of the design. Turn under the raw edges by 1.5cm (⅝in) and tack (baste) down. Measure the height of the embroidered patch and add 5cm (2in) to this measurement. Measure around the jar circumference and add 5cm (2in). Cut two pieces of gingham or patterned fabric using these measurements. Centralize the patch on to one of the band pieces and tack (baste) in place. Sew the patch on to the band and remove the tacking.

3 Make the band by placing the two gingham fabric pieces right sides together. Join together along the top and bottom edges with a 1.5cm (⅝in) seam. Turn the band to the right side and press. Turn 1.5cm (⅝in) of the raw edges under to the wrong side and press. Wrap the band around the jar, overlapping one end, and pin in position. Remove from the jar, sew the ends together, remove pins and slip the band on to the jar.

4 To make the jar cover, measure the diameter of the jar top and add 8cm (3in). Cut a circle of patterned fabric using this measurement. Place on top of the jar and secure with a rubber band or thin ribbon.

'Years ago, in a remnant of ancient sun worship, jams and sauces were always stirred sun wise – even millstones ran with the sun and a left-handed mill was very rare.'

Apples Pot Holder

Stitch count
53h x 52w

Design size
9.5 x 9.5cm (3¾ x 3¾in)

You will need
✧ 14.5 x 14.5cm (5¾ x 5¾in)
   cream 14-count Aida
✧ Tapestry needle size 24
✧ DMC stranded cotton as
   listed in the chart key
✧ Ready-made pot holder

If making a pot holder you will need:
✧ Two pieces of gingham
   21 x 21cm (8¼ x 8¼in)
✧ Bias binding 1.25m (1¼yd)
✧ Thick heat-proof wadding
   21 x 21cm (8¼ x 8¼in)

1 Stitch the design from the chart opposite in the centre of the Aida fabric using two strands of stranded cotton for cross stitch.

2 Trim the embroidery 2cm (¾in) beyond the widest measurements of the design shape. Turn under the raw edges by 1.5cm (⅝in) and tack (baste) down. Centralize the patch on to a ready-made pot holder and stitch around all sides, removing the tacking when finished.

If making your own pot holder

1 Place the two 21 x 21cm (8¼ x 8¼in) fabric pieces wrong sides together with the wadding between them and pin or tack (baste) the layers together. Sew together around all sides 1cm (⅜in) from the edge and then remove the pins or tacking.

2 Beginning at the top left corner, pin the bias binding around the edge of the pot holder and tack in place. Make a hanging loop by leaving 10cm (4in) of binding at the end. Fold the binding over the edge of the pot holder and sew in place by hand, starting at top left and ending by sewing the loop binding through all thicknesses. Fold this excess in half to the wrong side and sew the end down.

Fruity Tea Towel

Stitch count
24h x 68w

Design size
4.5 x 13.3cm (1¾ x 5¼in)

To decorate a tea towel you will need 5cm (2in) wide cream Aida band 26 stitches wide. Cut a length 5cm (2in) longer than the width of your towel. Stitch the design charted opposite over one block, beginning from the centre of the band and working outwards, using two strands of stranded cotton for cross stitch. Turn under the raw edges of the band by 1cm (⅜in) and tack (baste) down. Centralize the band on the tea towel, turn the edges over to the wrong side of the towel and tack into position. Stitch around the edges of the band and then remove tacking.

Jar Band

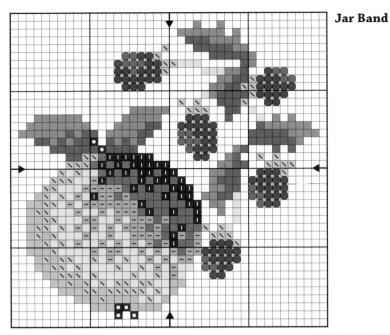

Pot Holder

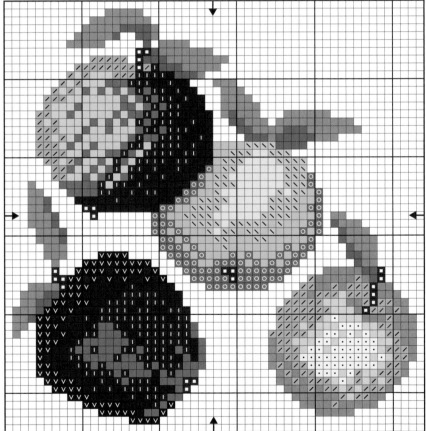

Baking Day Collection

DMC stranded cotton
Cross stitch

				French knots	
⊡	154	▨	742	⬤	154
☐	165	╱	743	⬤	3835
◥	166	☐	744		
■	347	⊡	3031		
I	350	•	3078		
▨	352	▨	3345		
–	353	▨	3347		
V	498	▨	3746		
○	580	▨	3834		
☐	581	–	3835		

Note: you will not need all of the
colours for the individual designs so
check the chart before you buy threads

Tea Towel

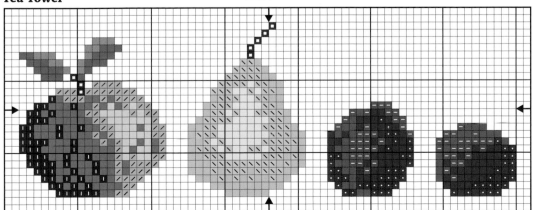

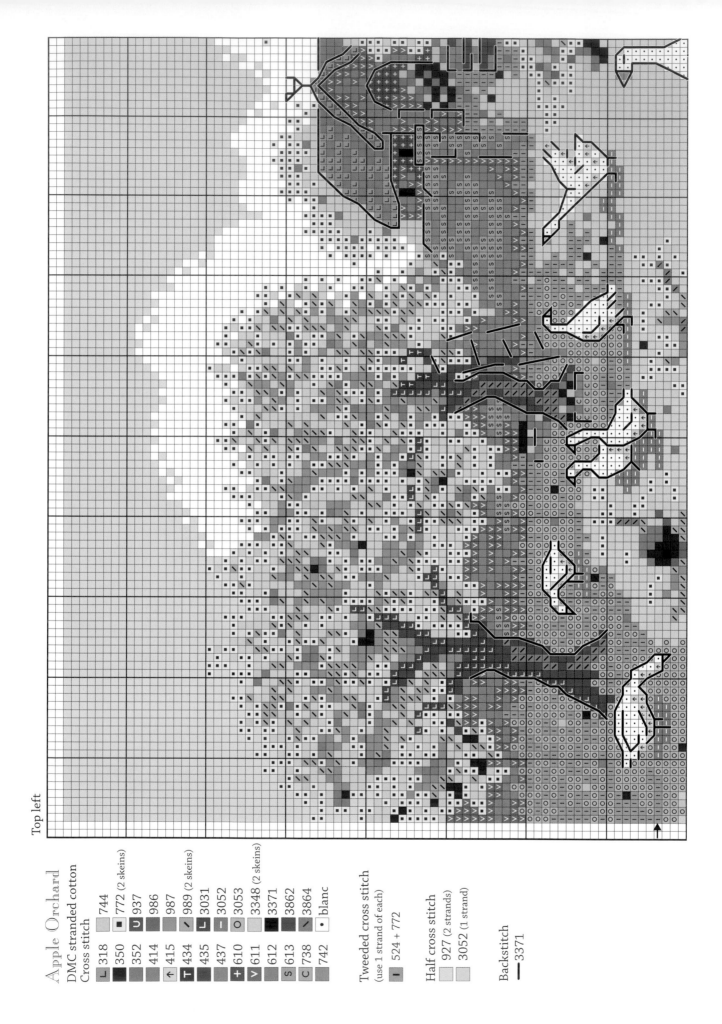

Top left

Apple Orchard
DMC stranded cotton
Cross stitch

∟	318		744
	350	■	772 (2 skeins)
	352	∪	937
	414		986
	415		987
←	434	↗	989 (2 skeins)
T	434	∟	3031
	435	−	3052
	437	○	3053
+	610		3348 (2 skeins)
V	611		3371
	612		3862
S	613	/	3864
C	738	•	blanc
	742		

Tweeded cross stitch
(use 1 strand of each)

I	524 + 772

Half cross stitch

	927 (2 strands)
	3052 (1 strand)

Backstitch

—	3371

— 14 —

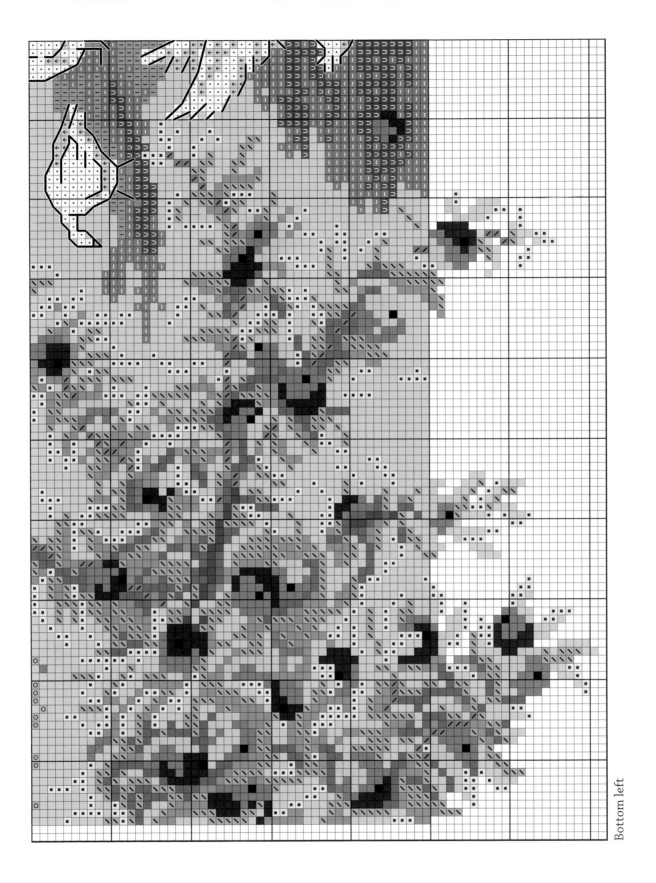

Apple Orchard

DMC stranded cotton

Cross stitch

∟	318	744
		350	772 (2 skeins)
∪	352	937
	414	986
↑	415	987
T	434	989 (2 skeins)
∟	435	3031
–	437	3052
+	610	3053
∨	611	3348 (2 skeins)
	612	3371
s	613	3862
c	738	3864
∕	742	blanc

Tweeded cross stitch
(use 1 strand of each)

∣	524 + 772

Half cross stitch

	927 (2 strands)
	3052 (1 strand)

Backstitch

——	3371

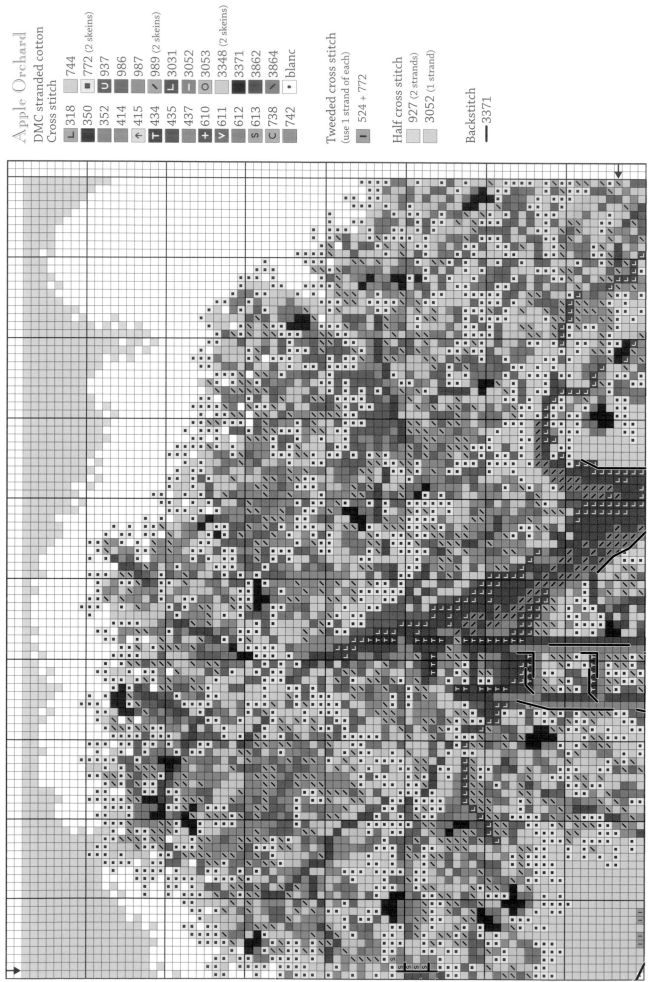

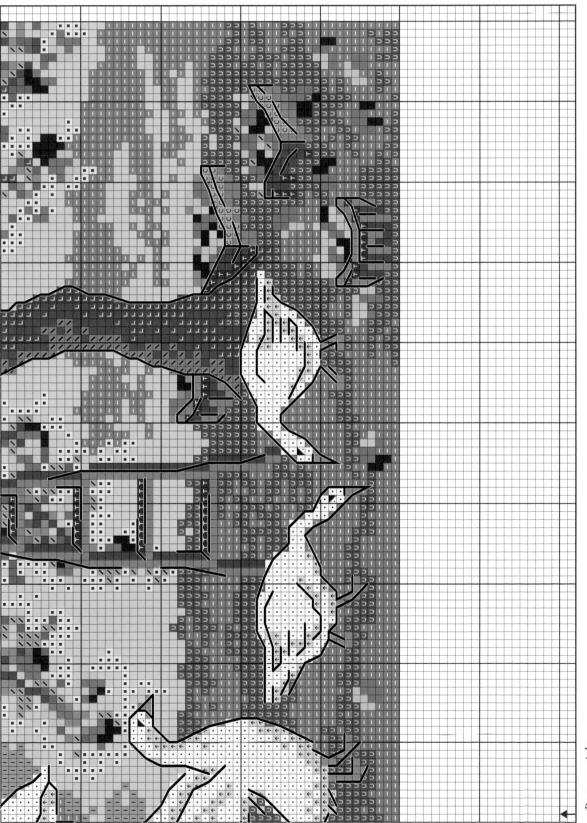

Designed by Carol Thornton

AT THE HARBOUR

This evocative design was inspired by Cornish and Devonshire fishing villages, where life revolved around the fishing industry, particularly the plentiful shoals of mackerel, pilchards and herring. Today the hustle and bustle of these ports, crowded with fishing boats, is diminished but the atmosphere is recalled in this scene.

Outside a traditional fisherman's cottage sits an old salt mending his nets. Around him little houses perch on steep and narrow cobblestone streets. Clinker-built boats bob on their moorings while the raucous cries of ever-greedy gulls fill the air. Years ago fishing nets were made from cord steeped in bark to make them waterproof; today bright, super-tough nylon is used. This old sailor wears the traditional cap and wool jersey. For generations these oiled-wool jerseys, lovingly knitted by fishermen's wives, repelled water and gave the men some protection from the blustering elements. The knitting patterns used echoed the sea, and included herringbone designs and wave patterns.

Fishing will always be a time-honoured occupation and in some quiet coastal village you will still stumble across a scene such as this, where a fisherman prepares once more to reap the harvest of the seas.

"MACKEREL SKIES AND MARE'S TAILS, MAKE SHIPS CARRY LOWERED SAILS."

In this picturesque scene, the afternoon sun is sinking in the sky, casting a warm glow on the solid harbour stones. A few scattered clouds promise fair weather on the morrow and, hopefully, a fine catch.

Harbourside Picture

This detailed scene conveys the timeless charm of an old village harbour with a warm range of shades used for the village and the sturdily built harbour and brighter colours for the boats.

STITCH COUNT
150h x 200w

DESIGN SIZE
27.2 x 36.2cm (10¾ x 14¼in)

YOU WILL NEED
✧ 42 x 51cm (16½ x 20in) white 14-count Aida
✧ Tapestry needle size 24
✧ DMC stranded cotton (floss) as listed in the chart key
✧ Suitable picture frame

The fisherman breathes
deep the evening air

The salt-smell, the reeds,
the sandy shore,

And with his hands deeply
lined with time and care

Gathers up his nets to
throw once more.

(from 'Fisherman at Eve'
by Sophia White)

1 Prepare your fabric for work (see page 96). Find and mark the centre of the fabric and the centre of the chart on pages 24–27. For your own use you could photocopy the chart parts and tape them together. Note: some colours use more than one skein – see the chart key for details. Mount your fabric in an embroidery frame if you wish.

2 Start stitching from the centre of the chart working outwards over one block of Aida. Use two strands of stranded cotton for full and three-quarter cross stitches and one strand for backstitches (you could work long stitches if preferred).

3 Once all the stitching is complete, frame the design as a picture (see page 100) or make up in some other way of your choice.

" SUNDAY SAIL,
NEVER FAIL;
FRIDAY SAIL,
ILL LUCK, GALE. "

Grilled Mackerel with Gooseberries

✧ Cook 200g (8oz) of gooseberries in a pan with a little butter until soft. Purée the fruit, sieve and place in a clean pan.

✧ Grill two filleted mackerels until cooked on both sides.

✧ Add a beaten egg to the gooseberry puree, reheat, add seasoning and then serve with the grilled mackerel and a green salad.

Nicely Nautical

Two smaller projects have been created using the harbour scene as inspiration – a useful drawstring bag for toiletries or cosmetics featuring a jaunty sailing boat and a face cloth decorated with bright flags.

Sailboat Bag

Stitch count
70h x 56w

Design size
12.7 x 10.2cm (5 x 4in)

You will need
- 18 x 15cm (7 x 6in) white 14-count Aida
- Tapestry needle size 24
- DMC stranded cotton (floss) as listed in chart key
- Two tea towels, one striped and one checked
- White cotton cord for drawstring 2m (2yd)
- White sewing thread

1 Stitch the design from the chart opposite on the Aida fabric using two strands of stranded cotton for cross stitch and one strand for backstitch. If preferred, you can omit the white cross stitch background.

2 To make the bag, cut the edges from both tea towels to make two pieces of fabric 67 x 30.5cm (26½ x 12in). Taking the outer striped towel (with stripes lengthways) fold in half so the right side is facing inwards and sew up the sides for 22.5cm (8¾in). Turn through to the right side, fold in the raw edges on the side gaps and hem.

These two designs make quick-stitch bathroom projects. The boat design would also make an attractive card, perhaps for Father's Day, while the flags could be used for a bookmark.

3 Fold the remaining check towel fabric in half and, again, with right sides facing, sew up either side, making this lining bag slightly smaller than the outer bag. Insert the outer striped bag into the smaller check bag, with right sides facing and with raw edges of the inner bag facing outwards on the outside. Match up side seams and sew the two bags together around the top, leaving a 10.2cm (4in) gap. Turn the bags right way out through the unstitched gap. Stitch up the gap. Arrange the bags neatly together and press. Form a channel for the drawstring by sewing around the bags twice – once 6cm (2½in) down from the top and then about 10.2cm (4in) from the top.

4 Attach the embroidery by first trimming the Aida to 15.2 x 12.7cm (6 x 5in). Turn under 1.3cm (½in) hems all round and press. Position the design on the bag and slipstitch in place. To finish, cut the white cord in half and feed into the drawstring channel from opposite sides, knotting the ends.

FLAGS FACE CLOTH

STITCH COUNT
168h x 10w (or length desired)
DESIGN SIZE
30.5 x 2cm (12 x ¾in)

To decorate a face cloth you will need a strip of white 14-count Aida 4.5 x 33cm (1¾ x 13in) and a white face cloth 30.5cm (12in) square. Stitch the design over one block, beginning from the centre of the strip and working outwards and using two strands of stranded cotton for cross stitch. Turn under the raw edges of the strip by 1.3cm (½in) all round, pin in place on the face cloth and stitch around the edges. Remove the pins when finished.

Boat and Flags
DMC stranded cotton
Cross stitch

	168
	350
╱	351
I	518
	611
	676
	677
╲	746
	798
	799
	800
	816
−	964
•	3799
	3808
	3810
+	3845
•	blanc

Backstitch
— 3799

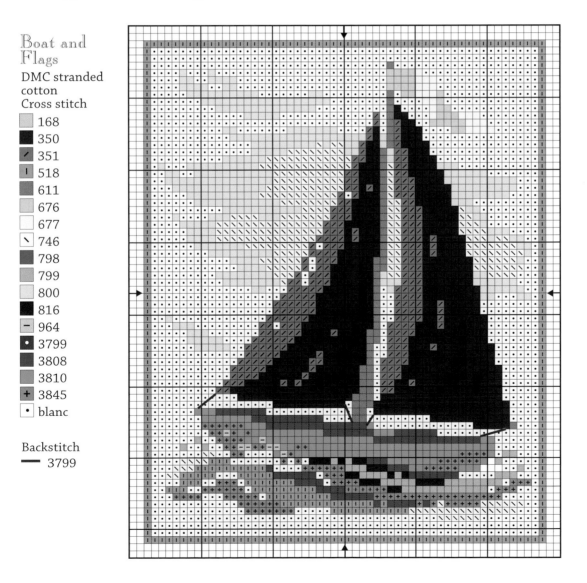

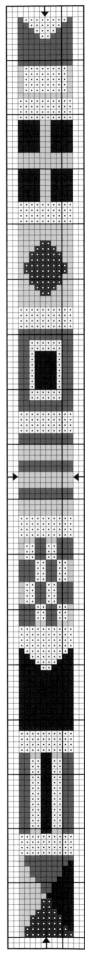

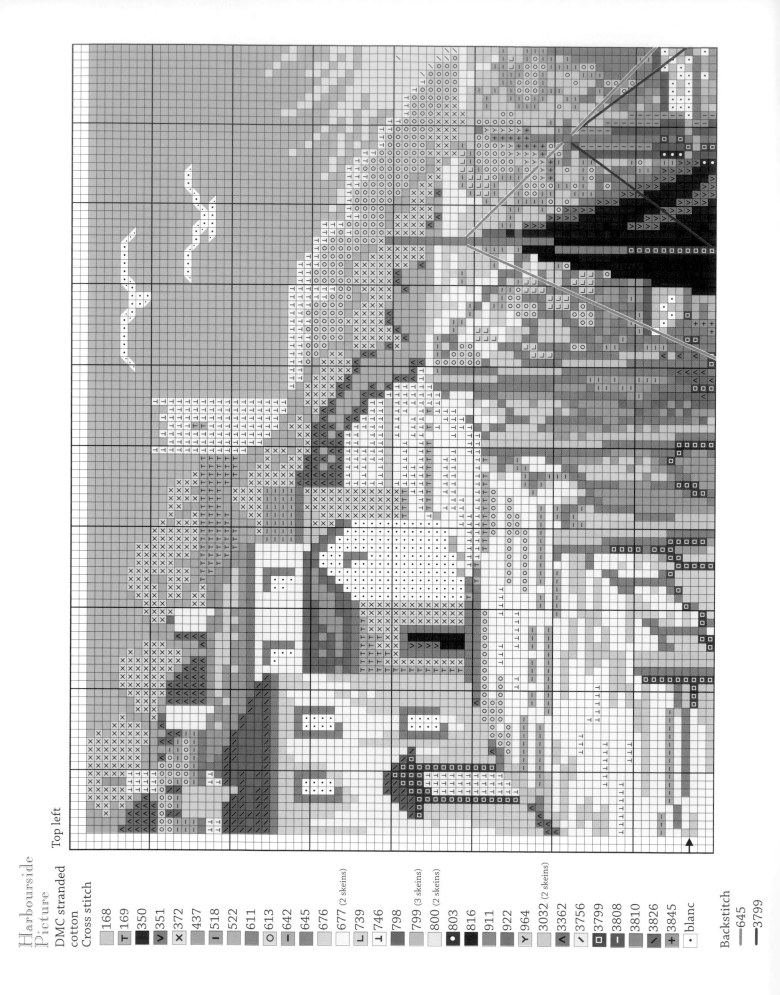

Harbourside Picture

Top left

DMC stranded cotton

Cross stitch

168	645	803	3362
T 169	676	816	< 3756
350	I 677 (2 skeins)	911	/ 3799
V 351	642	922	□ 3808
X 372	739	Y 964	I 3810
437	T 746	3032 (2 skeins)	3826
I 518	L 798		/ 3845
522	T 799 (3 skeins)		+ blanc
O 611	800 (2 skeins)		·
613	● 803		

Backstitch
— 645
— 3799

— 24 —

Bottom left

DMC stranded
cotton
Cross stitch

		168
T		169
		350
V		351
X		372
		437
–		518
		522
		611
		613
O		642
I		645
		676
		677 (2 skeins)
L		739
T		746
		798
		799 (3 skeins)
		800 (2 skeins)
●		803
		816
		911
		922
Y		964
<		3032 (2 skeins)
\		3362
□		3756
I		3799
		3808
/		3810
+		3826
		3845
·		blanc

Backstitch
—— 645
—— 3799

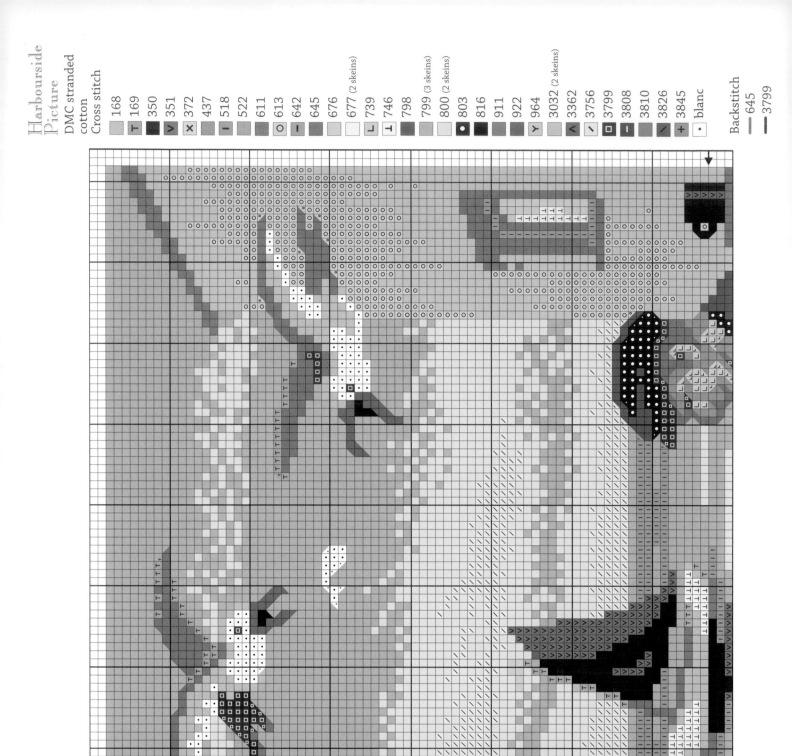

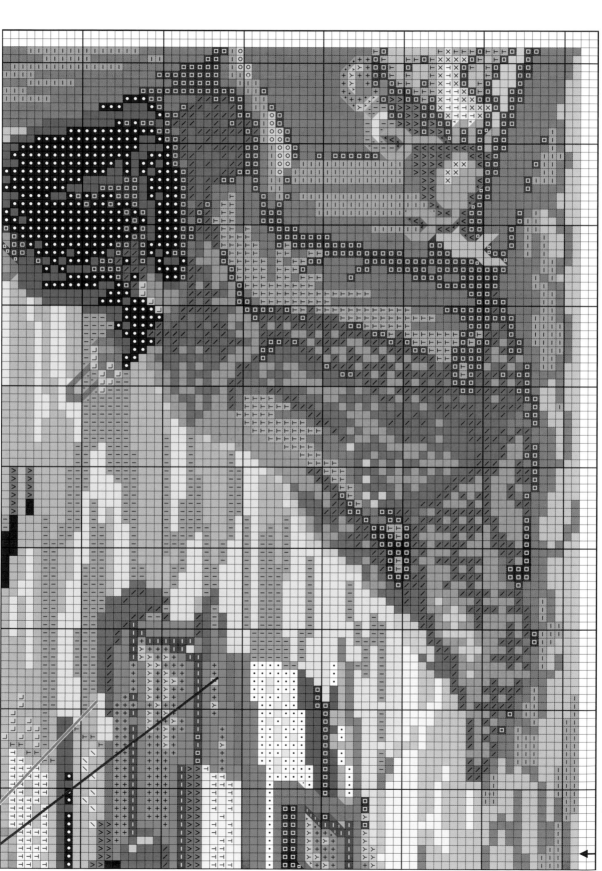

Bottom right

Designed by Caroline Palmer

BLUEBELL WOODS

*L*ate spring is bluebell time, when thousand upon thousand of these delicate belled flowers emerge from the detritus of winter and blossom en masse, stretching out in a dazzling display of azure blue. The dappled light of woodland is their favourite haunt and there can be no more beautiful a sight than their hazy blue carpet under a canopy of lime green beech leaves.

The bluebell is one of Britain's hardiest flowers, and its habit of returning year after year earned it the symbol of constancy in the Victorian language of flowers. Like that other perennial favourite, the primrose, it spreads readily, particularly in mixed woodlands, which are a haven for wildlife, rich as they are in a variety of plants – not just deciduous trees but bramble, nettle, gorse and other shrubs invaluable to animals and birds.

Wooded areas of Britain have diminished over the decades but the joyous sight of massed bluebells can still be seen in many counties of Britain. This evocative scene is a reminder that we only have to stray a little off the beaten path to find them.

"IF THE OAK'S BEFORE THE ASH,
YOU WILL ONLY GET A SPLASH,
BUT IF THE ASH PRECEDES THE OAK,
YOU WILL SURELY GET A SOAK."

This beautiful scene, with the azure haze of bluebells receding into the wood invites us to hop over the old-fashioned wooden stile and travel the path through the woodland canopy.

BLUEBELL PATH PICTURE

This beautiful picture would also look stunning made up as a wall hanging, especially if bordered by a print fabric to enhance the design. The light green Aida fabric the design is stitched on is important to produce the hazy background, creating the delightful impression that the wood goes on and on. To make up the charming bluebell greetings card shown below, see page 32.

STITCH COUNT
200h x 159w

DESIGN SIZE
36.3 x 29cm (14¼ x 11½in)

YOU WILL NEED
✧ 51 x 40.5cm (20 x 16in)
    light green 14-count Aida
    (DMC code 772)
✧ Tapestry needle size 24–26
✧ DMC stranded cotton (floss)
    as listed in the chart key
✧ Suitable picture frame

"WHEN LEAVES SHOW THEIR UNDERSIDES, BE VERY SURE THAT RAIN BETIDES."

1 Prepare your fabric for work (see page 96). Find and mark the centre of the fabric and the centre of the chart on pages 34–37. For your own use you could photocopy the chart parts and tape them together. Note: some colours use more than one skein – see chart key for details. Mount your fabric in an embroidery frame if you wish.

2 Start stitching from the centre of the chart working outwards over one block of Aida (or two threads of linen). Use two strands of stranded cotton for cross stitches and one for backstitches. The backstitches use a 'sketchy' style, which doesn't always follow the cross stitch exactly.

3 Once all the stitching is complete, make up as a picture (see page 100).

'The bluebell is the sweetest flower

That waves in summer rain:

Its blossoms have the mightiest power

To soothe my spirit's care.'

(Emily Brontë)

WOODLAND GREETINGS

This pretty set of designs inspired by life within a bluebell wood make delightful greetings cards for any occasion and can be embellished in any way you prefer. The cards are stitched and made up in a similar way – see the charts for the stitch counts and design sizes.

WOODLAND CARDS

YOU WILL NEED

◇ 15.2 x 12.7cm (6 x 5in) light green 14-count Aida (DMC code 772)
◇ Tapestry needle size 24–26
◇ DMC stranded cotton (floss) as listed in the chart key
◇ Double-fold card with a 10.2cm (4in) aperture to fit embroidery (see Suppliers)
◇ Small piece of wadding (batting)
◇ Double-sided adhesive tape
◇ Embellishments as desired

These lovely designs could be used in many other ways, perhaps as a collection of little pictures or as a set of coasters or as patches fixed to book covers.

1 Stitch the design charted opposite in the centre of the fabric, using two strands of stranded cotton for cross stitch and one for backstitch.

2 Once all stitching is complete, mount the embroidery into the card following the instructions on page 101. Add embellishments as desired.

3 To make a decorative cord plait three 60cm (24in) lengths of six-stranded embroidery thread. Slip the plait over the spine of the card, knot the ends and tease out the threads for a mini tassel. The bluebell card uses Anchor Multicolor thread 1335 for the cord, the wren card uses DMC Color Variations 1345 and the primrose card uses DMC Color Variations 4050. Stick-on ceramic charms add a pretty finishing touch (see Suppliers).

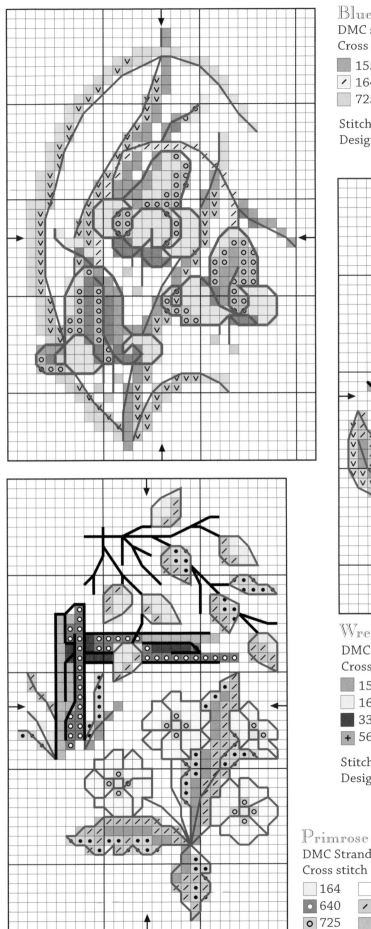

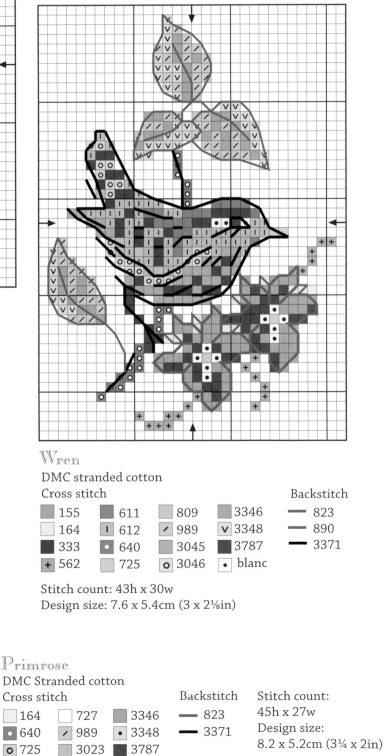

Bluebell

DMC stranded cotton

Cross stitch

155	800	3346
164	809	3348
725	989	3838

Backstitch

— 823
— 890

Stitch count 44h x 28w
Design size: 8 x 5cm (3⅛ x 2in)

Wren

DMC stranded cotton

Cross stitch

155	611	809	3346
164	612	989	3348
333	640	3045	3787
562	725	3046	blanc

Backstitch

— 823
— 890
— 3371

Stitch count: 43h x 30w
Design size: 7.6 x 5.4cm (3 x 2⅛in)

Primrose

DMC Stranded cotton

Cross stitch

164	727	3346
640	989	3348
725	3023	3787

Backstitch

— 823
— 3371

Stitch count:
45h x 27w
Design size:
8.2 x 5.2cm (3¼ x 2in)

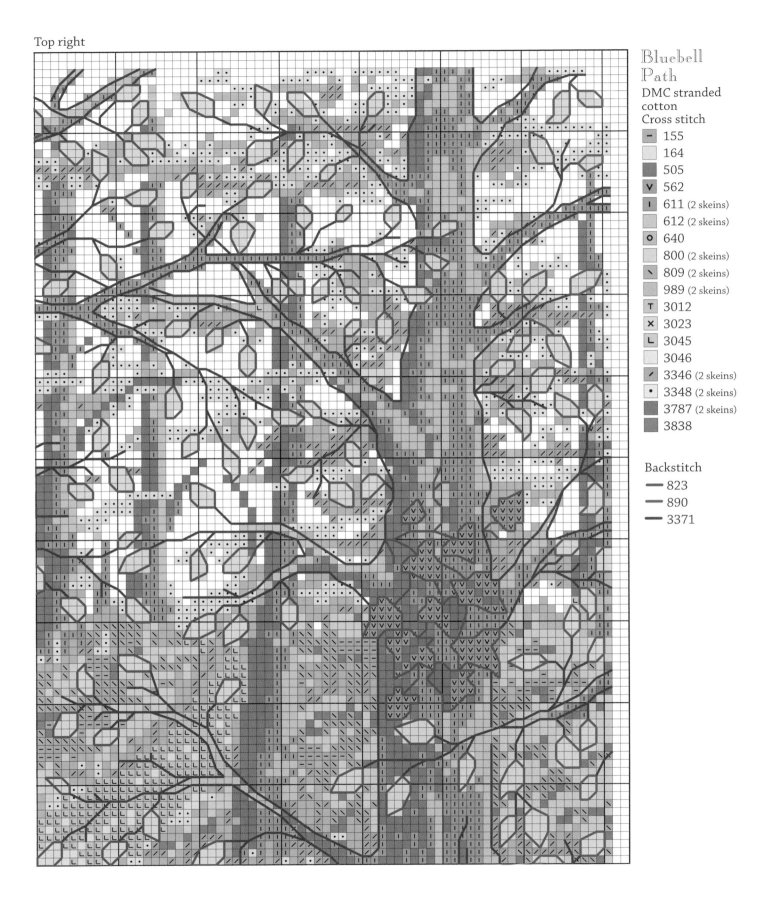

Bluebell Path

DMC stranded
cotton
Cross stitch

-	155
	164
	505
V	562
I	611 (2 skeins)
	612 (2 skeins)
O	640
	800 (2 skeins)
\	809 (2 skeins)
	989 (2 skeins)
T	3012
X	3023
L	3045
	3046
/	3346 (2 skeins)
·	3348 (2 skeins)
	3787 (2 skeins)
	3838

Backstitch

—	823
—	890
—	3371

Bottom left

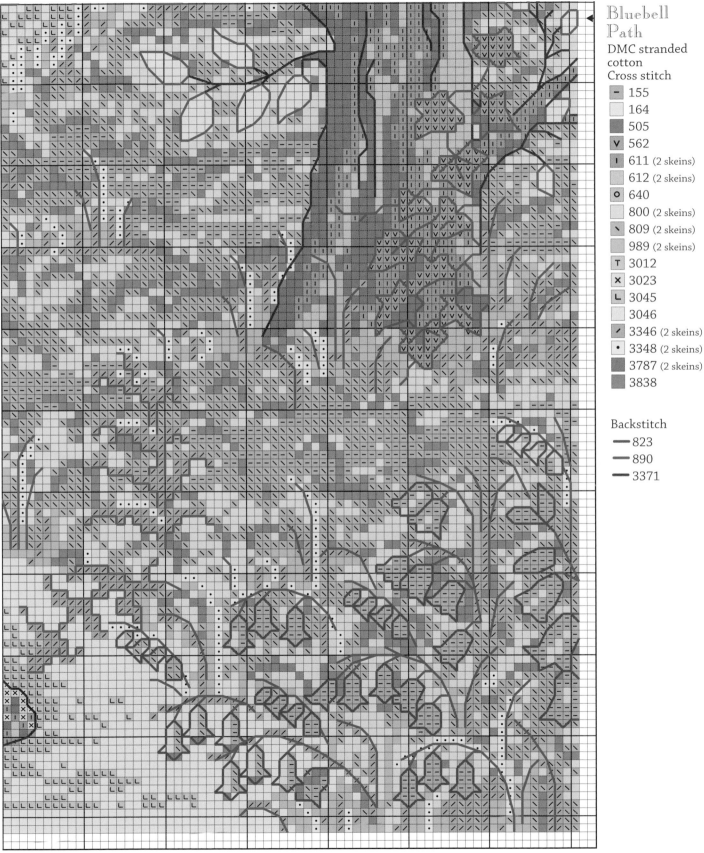

Bluebell
Path
DMC stranded
cotton
Cross stitch

- 155
  164
  505
v 562
I 611 (2 skeins)
  612 (2 skeins)
o 640
  800 (2 skeins)
\ 809 (2 skeins)
  989 (2 skeins)
T 3012
x 3023
L 3045
  3046
∕ 3346 (2 skeins)
• 3348 (2 skeins)
  3787 (2 skeins)
  3838

Backstitch
— 823
— 890
— 3371

Bottom right

Designed by Lesley Teare

Thatched Cottage

Nothing conveys bygone times quite like a thatched cottage, that idyllic country dwelling nestling intimately into its landscape. Thatched cottages were built for centuries and the dense, golden thatch was laid in tight bundles, often shaped into attractive patterns. The thatch might be made from wheat straw, reeds, rushes, grass or any other materials the thrifty cottager might have to hand.

These country cottages were invariably set amid a joyous garden full of sprawling, intermingled flowers and vegetables. Eternal favourites included vibrant poppy, rose and morning glory, tall spires of foxglove and hollyhock, the scented delights of lavender and pinks, plus hedgerow favourites of red campion and meadow cranesbill. Cottage gardens with their picturesque planting weren't just practical and beautiful but were also a haven for birds, bees, butterflies and all sorts of other wildlife.

We may not see thatched cottages being built today but more and more people hanker after the natural, at-one-with-nature life they convey. The red door of this delightful dwelling certainly beckons to us, drawing us past colourful flowers through the garden gate and on to the comforts within.

"A WINDY DAY IS NOT ONE FOR THATCHING."

This timeless scene is so attractive and full of colour and detail, with the cottage set in an atmospheric garden of lovely cottage garden flowers.

COUNTRY COTTAGE PICTURE

Little details bring this idyllic scene to life – a white cat sleeping on a bench in the sun and wisteria and clematis climbing the walls of the cottage. If you prefer, the design could be worked over two threads of a 28-count linen and would also make a stunning cushion.

STITCH COUNT
168h x 196w

DESIGN SIZE
30.5 x 35.5cm (12 x 14in)

YOU WILL NEED
✧ 46 x 51cm (20 x 18in) blue green 14-count Aida
✧ Tapestry needle size 24
✧ DMC stranded cotton (floss) as listed in the chart key
✧ Suitable picture frame

1 Prepare your fabric for work (see page 96). Find and mark the centre of the fabric and the centre of the chart on pages 48–51. For your own use you could photocopy the chart parts and tape them together. Mount your fabric in an embroidery frame if you wish.

2 Start stitching from the centre of the chart working outwards over one block of Aida (or two threads of linen). Use two strands of stranded cotton for full and three-quarter cross stitches. Use one strand for French knots, wound twice around the needle. Work backstitches (and any long stitches) with one strand. The backstitches are in a 'sketchy' style, which doesn't always follow the cross stitch exactly.

3 Once all the stitching is complete, frame the design as a picture (see page 100) or make up in some other way of your choice.

Homemade Rosewater

If you have a cottage-style garden with plenty of roses then rosewater is easy to make and can be used as a skin lotion or as a flavouring in cooking.

✧ Put three handfuls of fresh rose petals in a pan with 1 litre (2 pints) of mineral water.
✧ Simmer on low heat until the water is reduced by about half. Cool, strain and then bottle the liquid.

To make a skin lotion, mix rosewater, glycerine and lemon juice in equal quantities in a lidded container and shake well.

"WHERE FLOWERS BLOOM, SO DOES HOPE."

*'Flowers never emit so sweet and strong a fragrance
as before a storm. When a storm approaches thee,
be as fragrant as a sweet-smelling flower.'*
(Jean Paul Richter)

FLORAL GIFTS

These pretty projects feature some of the flowers found in a typical cottage garden – sweet pea, poppies and foxgloves. The items are decorated with dainty white lace and would make lovely gifts for friends and family.

FOXGLOVE JOURNAL

STITCH COUNT
67h x 49w

DESIGN SIZE
12 x 9cm (4¾ x 3½in)

YOU WILL NEED
✧ 23 x 20cm (9 x 8in) white 28-count linen
✧ Tapestry needle size 24
✧ DMC stranded cotton as listed in the chart key
✧ White lace 1m (1yd)
✧ Fast-tack fabric glue
✧ Double-sided adhesive tape
✧ Journal 16.5 x 21.5cm (6½ x 8½in)
✧ Sheet of card to match the journal

1 Stitch the complete design from page 46 over two threads of linen. Use two strands of stranded cotton for full and three-quarter cross stitches. Use one strand for French knots, wound twice around the needle. Work backstitches with one strand.

2 Once stitching is complete trim the edges of the embroidery to 14 squares either side of the design. Run a thin layer of fabric glue along the edges, place the lace on top of this and allow to dry.

3 Place the design on to your journal and fold the surplus fabric and lace to the back (inside) of the cover, trimming any excess not required. Secure in place with double-sided adhesive tape. Cut the card to fit the inside of the journal and glue in place to cover the fabric and neaten the inside.

*'Give me odorous at sunrise
a garden of beautiful flowers
where I can walk undisturbed.'*
(Walt Whitman)

These floral designs are quick to stitch and have been made up as a journal adornment, a bag and a scented sachet but the designs could be used in many different ways. For example, sew one to an apron as a patch or frame all three as pictures in matching frames.

Sweet Pea Sachet

Stitch count
40h x 36w (flowers only)
67h x 49w (whole design)

Design size
7 x 6.5cm (2¾ x 2½in) (flowers)
12 x 9cm (4¾ x 3½in) (whole)

You will need
✧ Two 18 x 18cm (7 x 7in)
   pieces of white 28-count
   linen (one for backing)
✧ Tapestry needle size 24
✧ DMC stranded cotton as listed
   in the chart key
✧ Gathered white lace
   0.5m (½yd)
✧ Pot-pourri or other filling

1 Stitch just the sweet pea flowers from the chart on page 47 over two threads of linen. If you wish to stitch the whole seed packet design you will need two larger pieces of fabric 25.4 x 20.3cm (10 x 8in). Use two strands of stranded cotton to work the full and three-quarter cross stitches. Use one strand for French knots, wound twice around the needle. Work backstitches with one strand.

2 Once stitching is complete, trim the fabric leaving 1.3cm (½in) all around the design. Cut a piece of backing linen the same size. Tack the gathered lace on to the edge of the back piece of linen with the lace facing inwards, towards the centre. Place the stitched design right side down on top, with the lace 'sandwiched' between, and machine or slipstitch around the edge. Leave a small gap for turning the sachet through to the right side.

3 Turn the sachet through to the right side and fill it with pot-pourri or other filling. Finish by slipstitching the opening closed.

" EACH FLOWER IS A SOUL
OPENING OUT TO NATURE"

'Many years ago flowers from cottage gardens, particularly pinks, roses, thyme and lad's love (artemesia) were picked, made into nosegays and sold to village lads for a halfpenny, to wear in their hats on Sundays.'

POPPY BAG

STITCH COUNT
67h x 49w

DESIGN SIZE
12 x 9cm (4¾ x 3½in)

YOU WILL NEED

✧ Two 20.3 x 12.7cm (8 x 5in)
  pieces of white 28-count
  linen (or size as required)
✧ Tapestry needle size 24
✧ DMC stranded cotton as
  listed in the chart key
✧ Gathered white lace
  0.5m (½yd)
✧ Narrow satin ribbon for a tie
✧ Lavender flowers to fill the
  bag (optional)

1 You can change the finished bag size
by cutting larger pieces of fabric. These
instructions are for the bag shown. Stitch the
design from page 47 over two threads of linen.
Use two strands of stranded cotton for full and
three-quarter cross stitches. Use one strand for
French knots, wound twice around the needle.
Work backstitches with one strand.

2 Once stitching is complete, tack (baste) a
piece of white lace to the right side of the
stitched fabric along the base edge, with the lace
facing inwards. Place the backing fabric on top of
the stitched design and machine or slipstitch the
sides and base together using a 1.3cm (½in) seam.

3 Turn the bag to the right side, turn the
top edges over by 1.3cm (½in) twice and
then hem. Slipstitch the gathered lace in place
along the top edge. To finish, tie the satin ribbon
around the neck of the bag in a bow.

Lavender Mint Tea

A cottage garden was sure to have a supply of
fragrant lavender and a patch or two of mint.
Both can be combined in a refreshing drink.

✧ For one cup of tea, take one heaped teaspoon of
  fresh lavender flowers and put in a teapot with
  two tablespoons of fresh mint leaves.
✧ Pour boiling water over and leave to steep for
  five minutes before pouring.

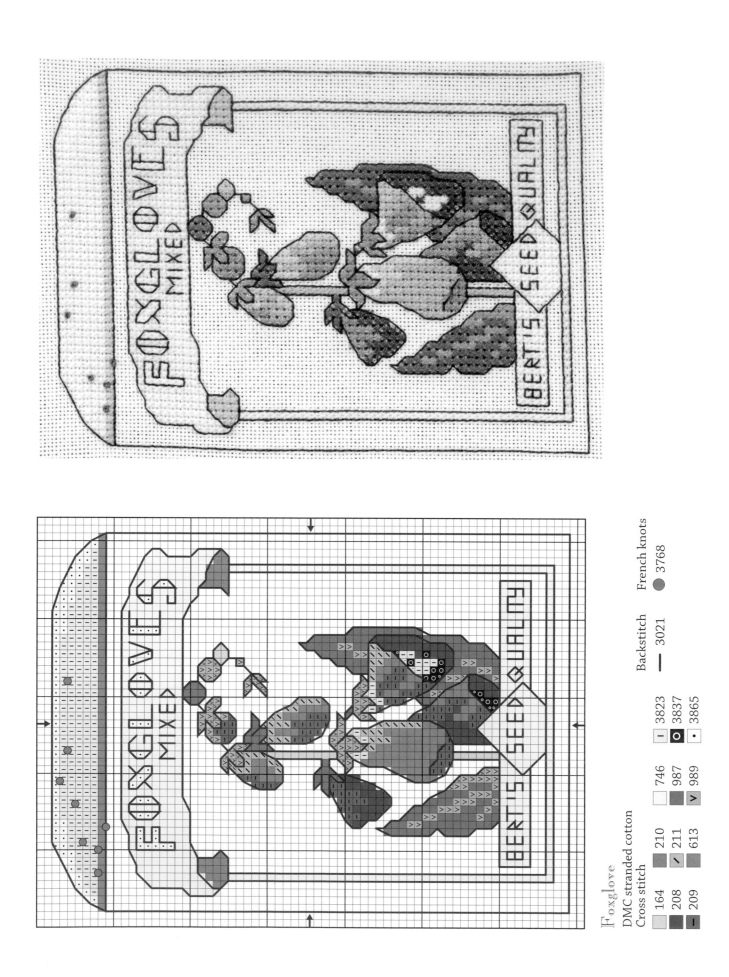

Foxglove

DMC stranded cotton
Cross stitch

164	746		–	3823
210	987		O	3837
208 ✓	211		•	3865
209 –	613	V	989	

Backstitch
— 3021

French knots
● 3768

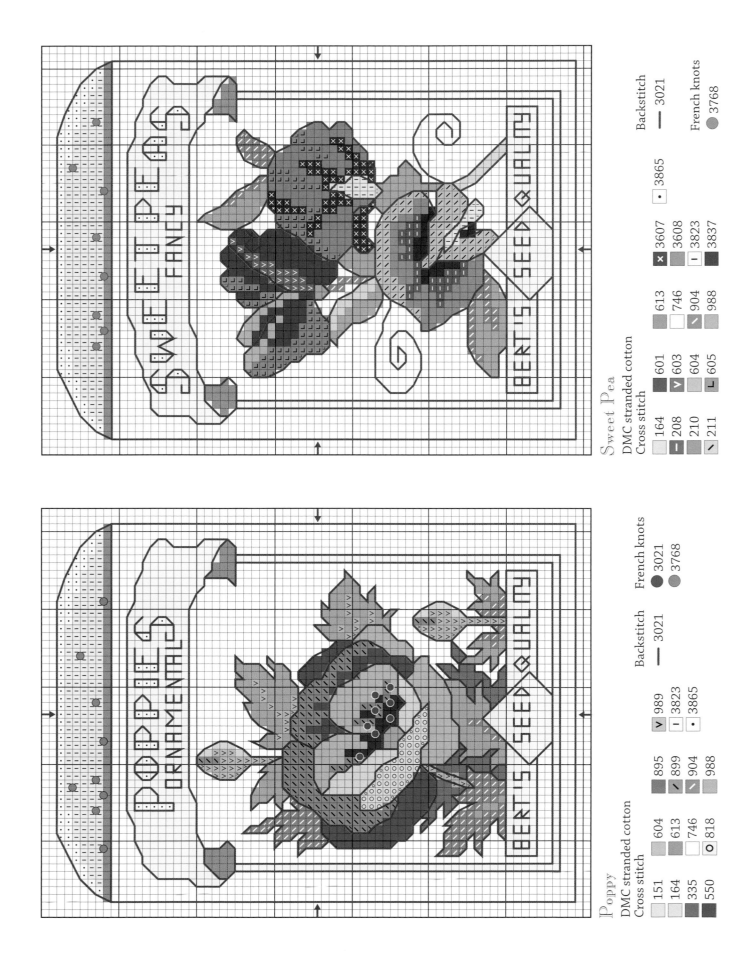

Sweet **P**ea

DMC stranded cotton
Cross stitch

	164		601		613	**Backstitch**
−	208	∨	603		746	—— 3021
	210		604	╱	904	
╱	211	∟	605		988	**French knots**
		×	3607	•	3865	● 3768
			3608			
		−	3823			
			3837			

Poppy

DMC stranded cotton
Cross stitch

	151		604	∨	989	**Backstitch**	**French knots**
	164		613	−	3823	—— 3021	● 3021
	335		746	•	3865		● 3768
	550	○	818				
			895				
		╱	899				
		╱	904				
			988				

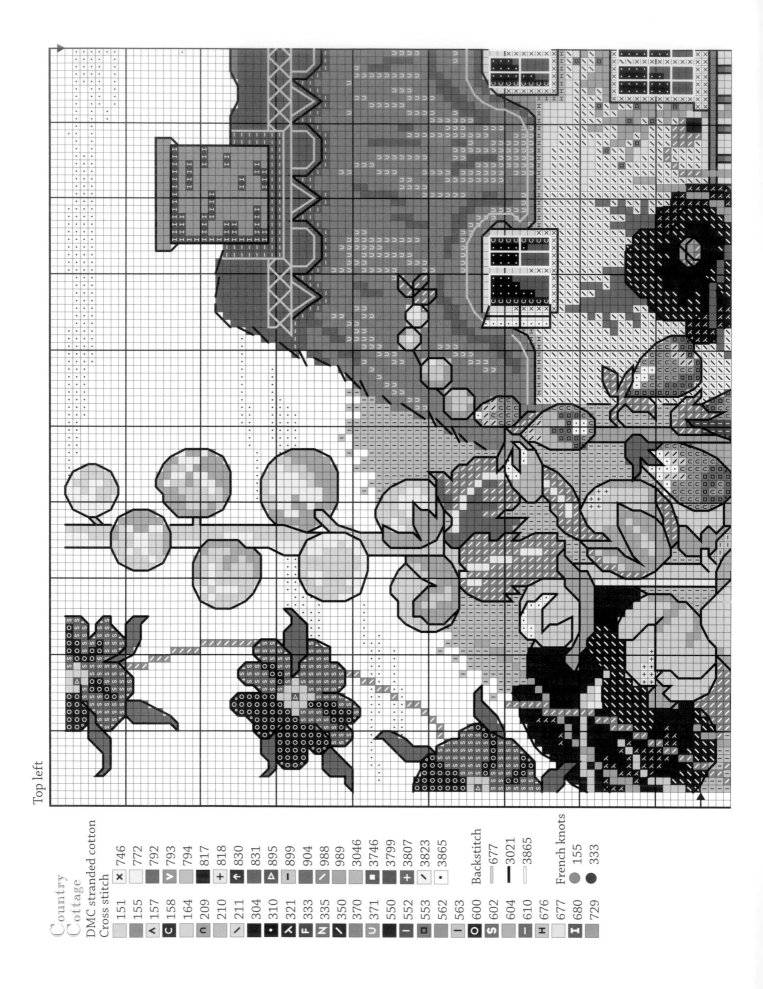

Country
Cottage

DMC stranded cotton
Cross stitch

✕	746				
	155				
◀	157				
⌂	158				
⌐	164				
	209				
	210				
+	211				
↙	304				
	310				
△	321				
❙	333				
⤢	335				
F	350				
Z	370				
╱	371				
∪	550				
■	552				
+	553				
╲	562				
•	563				
─	600				
Ⓞ	602				
S	604				
	610				
❙	676				
H	677				
❙	680				
	729				

792
793
794
817
818
830
831
895
899
904
988
989
3046
3746
3799
3807
3823
3865

Backstitch
——— 677
——— 3021
——— 3865

French knots
● 155
● 333

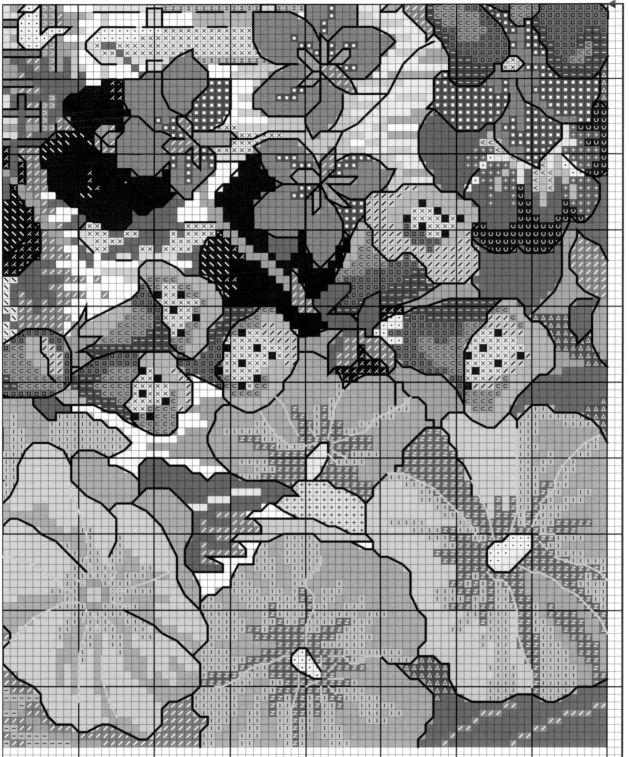

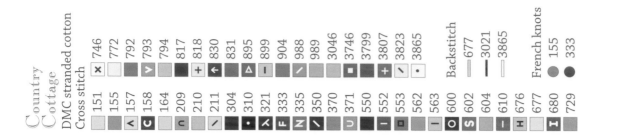

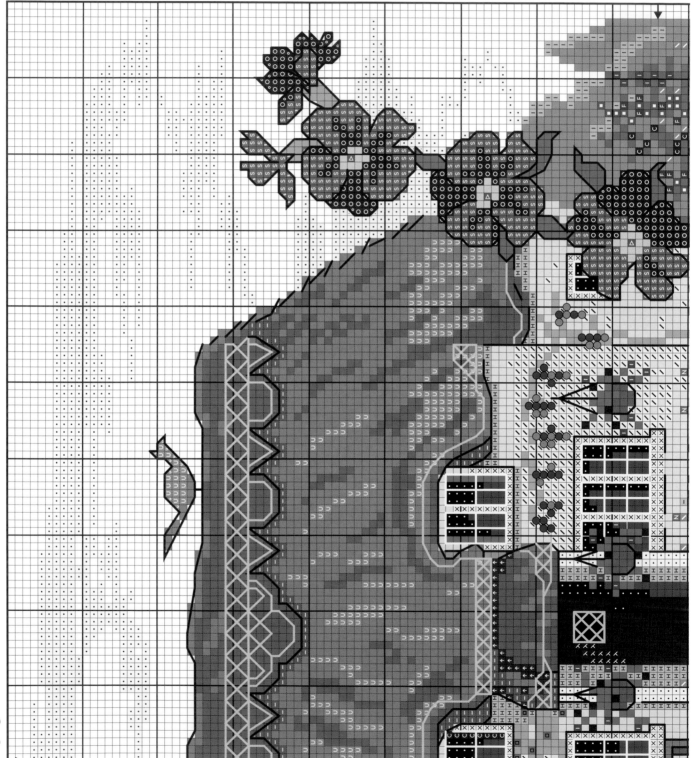

Designed by Caroline Palmer

Summer Skies

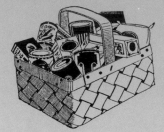

This idyllic country picnic scene amid rolling fields and hills conjures up so many pleasurable images, making you want to run carefree and barefoot through cool meadow grasses as the hot summer sun beats down. Fling down a blanket, lie full length in the sweet-scented pasture and watch the darting flight of swallows, or if you are lucky huge hot-air balloons rising into the blue, blue sky.

There is nothing more relaxing than being surrounded by the drowsy buzz of insects and the erratic flight of butterflies as they visit sweet clover and buttercups. All around there are brightly coloured meadow flowers – ox-eye daisies, gillyflowers, wild geraniums and cornflowers – all growing in profusion in the long, lush grass. And above them all the brilliant blaze of scarlet poppies, proud lords of the July fields.

The rolling countryside, verdant with high-summer growth, is still to be found all around us and we can still enjoy such rich, golden days – perhaps while holidaying in rural retreats, perhaps a few miles out of town, or perhaps as near as that little wildflower patch in our own back gardens.

"Rain before seven, fine before eleven;
evening red and morning grey –
two sure signs of one fine day."

All a country picnic really needs is a comfortable rug, a pitcher of cold lemonade, tasty sandwiches, fresh strawberries and acres of blue sky.

PICNIC PICTURE

This halcyon scene epitomizes the perfect summer afternoon, enjoying a delicious picnic in a wild flower meadow, hot sun overhead and the icing on the cake – a flotilla of colourful hot-air balloons. The colour of the Aida fabric is important to create the lovely blue sky.

STITCH COUNT
152h x 214w

DESIGN SIZE
27.5 x 38.8cm (10¾ x 15¼in)

YOU WILL NEED
✧ 40.6 x 51cm (16 x 20in) light blue 14-count Aida (DMC code 800)
✧ Tapestry needle size 24
✧ DMC stranded cotton (floss) as listed in the chart key
✧ Suitable picture frame

'Summer set lip to earth's bosom bare,

And left the flush'd print in a poppy there.

Like a yawn of fire from the grass it came,

And the fanning wind puff'd it to flapping flame.'

(from 'The Poppy' by Francis Thompson)

1 Prepare your fabric for work (see page 96). Find and mark the centre of the fabric and the centre of the chart on pages 62–65. For your own use you could photocopy the chart parts and tape them together. Note: some colours use more than one skein – see the chart key for details. Mount your fabric in an embroidery frame if you wish.

2 Start stitching from the centre of the chart working outwards over one block of Aida (or two threads of linen). Use two strands of stranded cotton for cross stitches and one strand for backstitches. The backstitches use a 'sketchy' style, which doesn't always follow the cross stitch exactly.

3 Once all the stitching is complete, frame the design as a picture (see page 100) or make up in some other way of your choice.

" A RAINBOW AFTERNOON, GOOD WEATHER COMING SOON. **"**

Homemade Lemonade

What picnic would be complete without some chilled wine or thirst-quenching homemade lemonade? The lemon syrup is also a tasty dressing for avocado.

✧ Grate the zest from four lemons into a large saucepan. Add the juice squeezed from the lemons and then cut the remains of the lemons into chunks and add these too. Add a teaspoon of citric or tartaric acid crystals, 400g (1lb) of sugar and 600ml (1 pint) of boiling water.
✧ Heat the mixture until all the sugar has dissolved, remove from the heat and leave overnight to steep.
✧ In the morning strain the lemon syrup, pressing out all of the liquid. Discard the pulp and bottle the golden liquid. Dilute to taste with chilled, sparkling spring water.

ALFRESCO COLLECTION

A simple picnic can be turned into a special event with this useful set of placemat, cutlery case and napkin holder. The blue linen creates an attractive contrast to the stitching. Making up is easier if you use a soft rather than a stiff linen.

POPPY PLACEMAT

STITCH COUNT
45h x 44w

DESIGN SIZE
8.2 x 8.2cm (3¼ x 3¼in)

YOU WILL NEED
- 28 x 40.5cm (11 x 16in) light blue 28-count linen (DMC code 3840)
- Tapestry needle size 24–26
- DMC stranded cotton (floss) as listed in the chart key
- 28 x 40.5cm (11 x 16in) print backing fabric
- 28 x 40.5cm (11 x 16in) thin wadding (batting)
- Matching sewing thread

1 Prepare your fabric for work (see page 96). Stitch the design from the chart on page 61 over two threads of the linen fabric, using two strands of stranded cotton for cross stitch and one strand for backstitch. Position the poppy motif in a corner of the fabric, approximately 5cm (2in) from the right side and the top of the fabric.

2 Make up the placemat as follows. Remove any creases by placing the embroidery face down on to some thick towels and ironing on a medium setting. Iron the backing fabric if necessary (a cloudy sky print was used). Place the two pieces right sides together with the piece of wadding on top. Using 6mm (¼in) seams (or slightly wider if your linen frays very easily) sew all around the edges of the fabric and wadding 'sandwich', leaving a 10.2cm (4in) gap at the bottom.

3 Clip the corners and turn the placemat through to the right side, making sure that the corners are well turned out. Press the seams. Turn the edges of the gap under and slipstitch the edges together invisibly with matching thread. If desired, decorate the placemat by adding blanket stitch (see page 98) around the edge with three strands of off-white stranded cotton or other colour of your choice.

Some pretty print fabric can be used to line these three projects, which would also make the napkin holder and placemat reversible. Some chunky blanket stitch edging creates a rustic feel.

MEADOW CUTLERY CASE

1 Prepare your fabric for work (see page 96). Stitch the design from page 60 over two threads of the linen fabric in the position shown in the diagram, using two strands of stranded cotton for cross stitch and one strand for backstitch.

2 Make up the cutlery case as follows. Trim the embroidered fabric to 51 x 12.7cm (20 x 5in). Place the embroidered piece and the lining piece right sides together with the piece of wadding on top and pin. Using a small glass, draw pencil curves at the bottom corners (see diagram). Using 6mm (¼in) seams (or slightly wider if your linen frays very easily) sew all around the edges of the fabric sandwich, leaving the top open.

3 Trim the curved seams and turn the case through to the right side, making sure that the curves are well turned out (use a wooden spoon to reach them). Press the seams. Using matching thread, stitch one half of the popper fastener about 2.5cm (1in) down from the gap. Turn the edges of the gap under and slipstitch together with matching sewing thread. Sew on the top half of the popper from the lining side of the flap, sewing a decorative button on the other side of the flap at the same time.

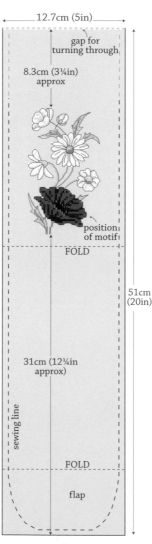

Position of the cross stitch motif on the fabric 'sandwich'

4 Fold the bottom part of the case up by about 20cm (8in) as indicated by the fold line on the diagram and slipstitch the side edges together neatly with matching thread.

5 Decorate the case by adding blanket stitch (see page 98) all around using three strands of an off-white stranded cotton. Start at the bottom left, work up one side, around the top curve and then down the other side. Add a row of blanket stitch along the opening of the case to finish.

Daisy Napkin Holder

Stitch count
39h x 39w

Design size
7 x 7cm (2¾ x 2¾in)

You will need
◆ 20.5 x 33cm (8 x 13in) light blue
   28-count linen (DMC code 3840)
◆ Tapestry needle size 24–26
◆ DMC stranded cotton (floss)
   as listed in the chart key
◆ 11.5 x 23cm (4½ x 9in) lining fabric
◆ 11.5 x 23cm (4½ x 9in) thin
   wadding (batting)
◆ Two pieces of decorative ribbon
   each 35cm (14in) long
◆ Two decorative buttons
◆ Matching sewing thread

1 Prepare your fabric for work (see page 96). Stitch the design from page 61 over two threads of the linen fabric in the position shown in the diagram below, using two strands of stranded cotton for cross stitch and one for backstitch.

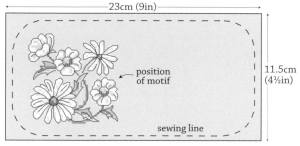

23cm (9in)

position
of motif

11.5cm
(4½in)

sewing line

*Position of the cross stitch
motif on the fabric 'sandwich'*

2 Make up the napkin holder as follows. Trim the embroidered fabric to 11.5 x 23cm (4½ x 9in). Place the embroidered piece and the lining piece right sides together with the wadding on top and pin. Using a small glass or coin, draw pencil curves at the four corners. Using 6mm (¼in) seams (or slightly wider if your linen frays very easily) sew all around the edges of the fabric sandwich, leaving a 7.6cm (3in) gap in one side.

3 Clip the curved corners and turn the holder through to the right side, making sure that the curves are well turned out. Press the seams. Turn the edges of the gap under and slipstitch together invisibly with matching sewing thread.

4 Attach the ribbon ties by hemming one end of a piece of ribbon and sewing it in place on the reverse side of the holder, adding a decorative button to cover the ribbon end. Repeat for the other side. Sew in place *only* through the backing fabric and wadding, not through to the front of the embroidery. By sewing on the button and ribbon in this way, the napkin holder becomes reversible. Using three strands of off-white stranded cotton, work blanket stitch (see page 98) around all edges of the holder. To finish, wrap the holder around your napkin and tie the ribbons in a bow.

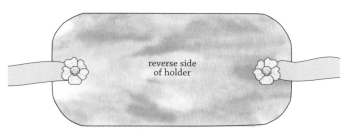

reverse side
of holder

*Sewing on the decorative buttons and
ribbon ties on the reverse of the holder*

Cutlery Case

DMC stranded cotton
Cross stitch

				Backstitch
◣ 164	▨ 725	▨ 989	▨ 3853	▬ 310
◙ 310	◉ 727	▨ 3705	✛ 3854	▬ 814
▨ 415	▨ 772	◤ 3831	• blanc	▬ 890

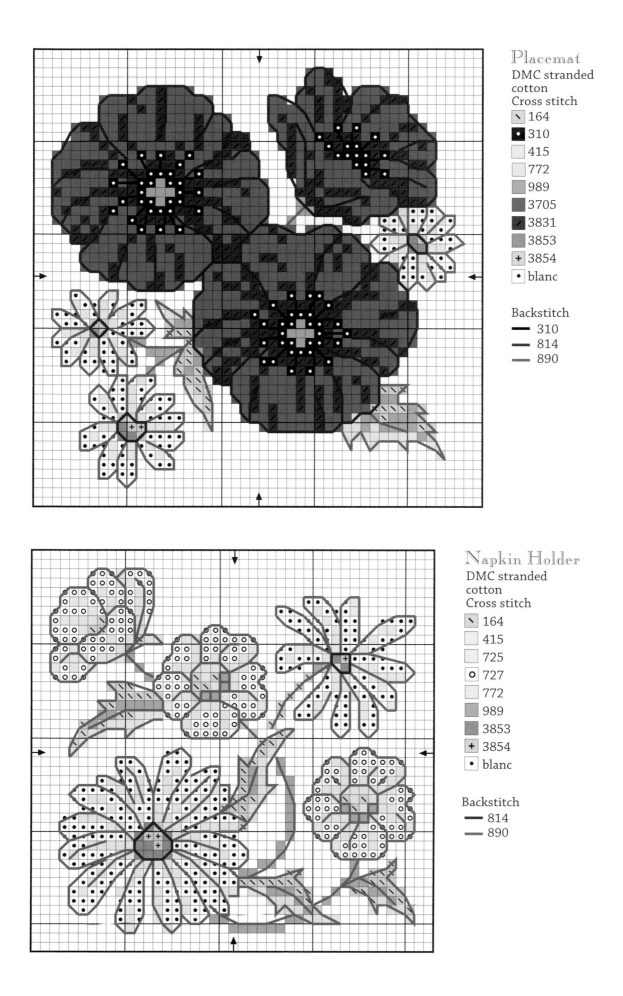

Placemat
DMC stranded cotton
Cross stitch

↘	164
■	310
	415
	772
	989
	3705
◧	3831
	3853
+	3854
•	blanc

Backstitch
— 310
— 814
— 890

Napkin Holder
DMC stranded cotton
Cross stitch

↘	164
	415
	725
○	727
	772
	989
	3853
+	3854
•	blanc

Backstitch
— 814
— 890

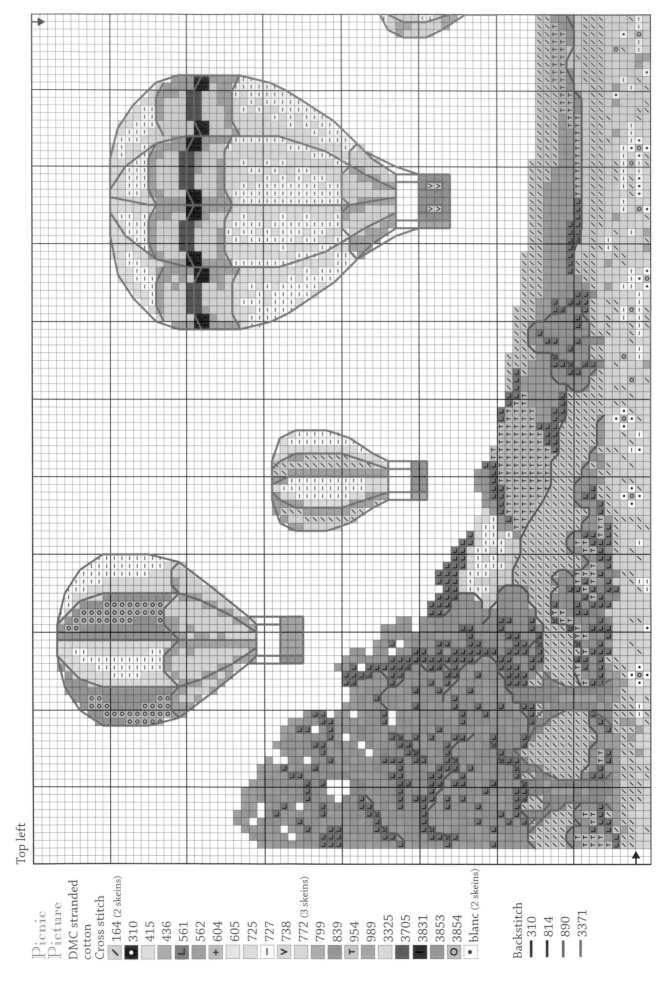

Picnic
Picture

DMC stranded
cotton

Cross stitch

╱	164 (2 skeins)
●	310
	415
	436
∟	561
	562
+	604
	605
	725
I	727
V	738
	772 (3 skeins)
	799
	839
T	954
	989
	3325
	3705
▬	3831
	3853
O	3854
•	blanc (2 skeins)

Backstitch

	310
	814
	890
	3371

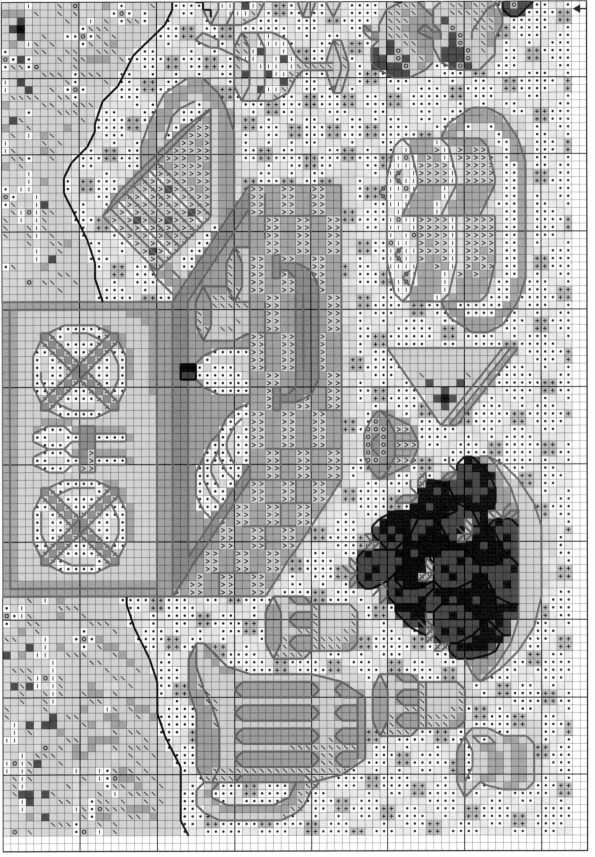

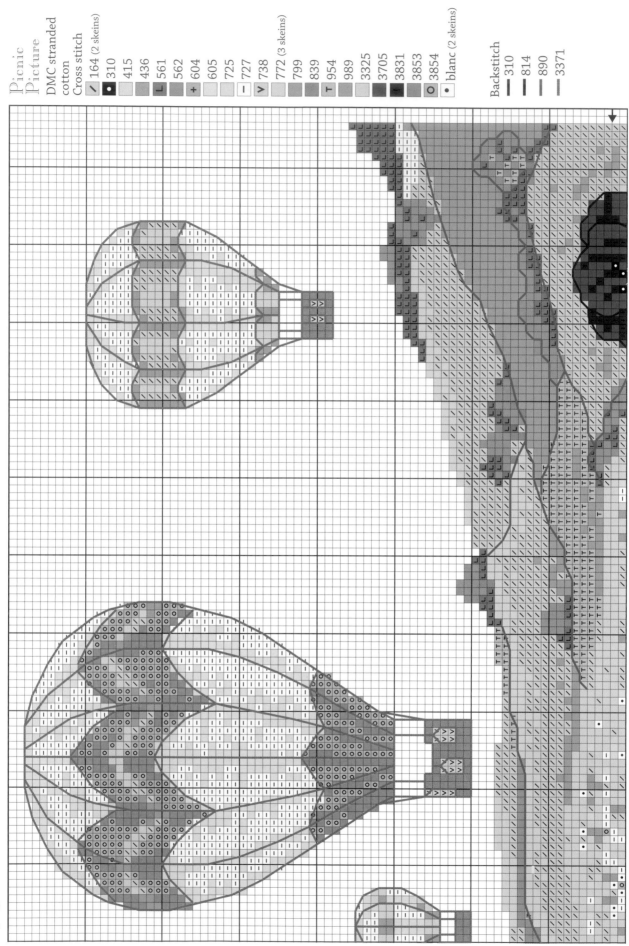

Top right

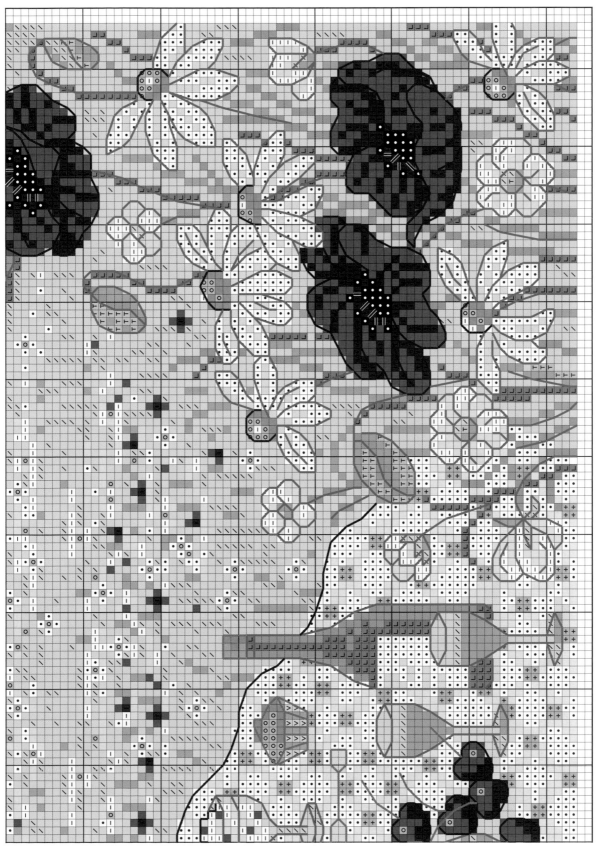

BY THE CANAL

Relaxing by the canal on a planked jetty, canal folk are settling in for a warm, drowsy afternoon. Perhaps tomorrow they will cast off and explore a few more miles of the canal ahead. This tranquil scene was inspired by places on the Peak Forest Canal in Derbyshire and the Rochdale Canal, which runs from Manchester in Lancashire through to West Yorkshire. Surrounded by trees, some brightly painted narrowboats invite us to climb aboard and explore.

Narrowboat painting originated as a distinctive British craft on the canals during the 19th century. Favourite motifs of this folk-art technique included stylized castles, ruins, roses and other flowers, all painted with enamel-bright primary colours – a tradition that continues today.

There may be few working barges left today but the canalways of Britain are still busy, a magnet for water-loving travellers floating the length and breadth of the country in these atmospheric narrowboats. The canal towpaths, originally trod by steady horses as they pulled barges laden with coal, cereals and timber, are also visited by lovers of the countryside keen to walk and cycle along their quiet ways.

**"WHEN WINDOWS WON'T OPEN,
AND THE SALT CLOGS THE SHAKER,
THE WEATHER WILL FAVOUR
THE UMBRELLA MAKER"**

This scene invites us to the peace and quiet of the waterways, where distinctive narrowboats are colourfully reflected in the calm water of the canal.

CANAL LIFE PICTURE

This peaceful canal-side scene is filled with colourful details and will be a relaxing picture to stitch, as well as to admire. There are also designs for two smaller projects, a napkin and placemat, their style deliberately naive and reminiscent of French folk art.

STITCH COUNT
150h x 200w

DESIGN SIZE
27.2 x 36.3cm (10¾ x 14¼in)

YOU WILL NEED
- 40.5 x 48cm (16 x 19in) white 14-count Aida
- Tapestry needle size 24–26
- DMC stranded cotton (floss) as listed in the chart key
- Suitable picture frame

" COLD IS THE NIGHT
WHEN THE STARS
SHINE BRIGHT. "

1 Prepare your fabric for work (see page 96). Find and mark the centre of the fabric and the centre of the chart on pages 72–75. For your own use you could photocopy the chart parts and tape them together. Note: some colours use more than one skein – see the chart key for details. Mount your fabric in an embroidery frame if you wish.

2 Start stitching from the centre of the chart working outwards over one block of Aida (or two threads of linen). Use two strands of stranded cotton for full and three-quarter cross stitches and one strand for backstitches (note: the backstitches only occur in two places).

3 Once all the stitching is complete, frame the design as a picture (see page 100) or make up in some other way of your choice.

'The workmen who excavated the English canals from 1755 onwards were called navigators (shortened to 'navvies'), because canals were regarded as inland navigation lines. The term is still used for a hard-working labourer.'

Navvy's Stew

The navigators or 'navvies' who built the network of canals worked hard and needed hearty meals to sustain them and this stew would fit the bill.

✧ Cut 2kg (1lb) of beef (brisket or shin) into chunks, toss in flour and fry in oil until brown.

✧ Add the beef to a large saucepan with roughly chopped onions, carrots, potato, swede (or turnip), field mushrooms, a handful of dried pearl barley and a handful of dried red lentils.

✧ Just cover the ingredients with hot water (or stock), plus a glass of Guinness or dark beer. Season and then simmer slowly for two hours, stirring occasionally. Serve the stew with large wedges of crusty bread.

Canal Collection

A rustic ploughman's lunch beside the canal or while chugging along in a colourful narrowboat would be all the more memorable with this cheerful placemat and napkin.

Flowers Placemat

STITCH COUNT
56h x 14w (for one repeat of the design)

DESIGN SIZE
10.2 x 2.5cm (4 x 1in)

This design is very quick to stitch. For a placemat with a depth of 30.5cm (12in), repeat the design opposite three times. Stitch on a 35.5 x 7.6cm (14 x 3in) strip of white 14-count Aida using two strands of stranded cotton for cross stitch, beginning 2.5cm (1in) from one end and repeating the design three times. Trim the embroidery to within 1.3cm (½in) of the edge of the stitching, fold back the unworked fabric around the edges and press. Cut a tea towel in half and trim to create two pieces of fabric 47 x 33.5cm (18½ x 13in). Sew the embroidery on 3.8cm (1½in) from the right-hand short edge of one piece. Place the two pieces of fabric right sides together, sew around the edge, leaving a gap for turning through. Turn to the right side, sew up the gap and press to finish.

*A row of simple flowers makes a pretty adornment to a placemat,
while a posy design creates a bright napkin. The posy would also
make a charming card.*

Posy Napkin

Stitch count
42h x 42w
Design size
7.6 x 7.6cm (3 x 3in)

A little posy of flowers has been stitched and used as a patch to decorate a napkin made from a bright red tea towel. Stitch the motif on a 12.7cm (5in) square of white 14-count Aida using two strands of stranded cotton for cross stitch. Trim the embroidery to 9cm (3½in) square, fold back the unworked fabric around the edges and press. Cut a 50cm (20in) square of fabric from a tea towel, or other fabric of your choice, and sew the posy patch in one corner, about 4cm (1½in) from the edges. Press to finish.

Placemat   **Napkin**

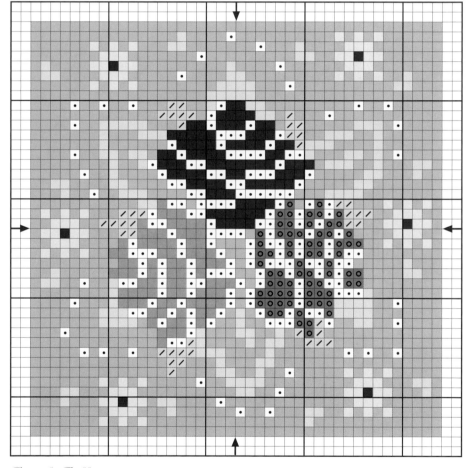

Canal Collection
DMC stranded cotton
Cross stitch

▨	316	◪ 523	
▨	334	▨ 789	
■	347	▨ 3813	
◉	351	▨ 3822	
▨	501	· blanc	

Stitch the placemat
design three times to fill
a 30.5cm (12in) placemat

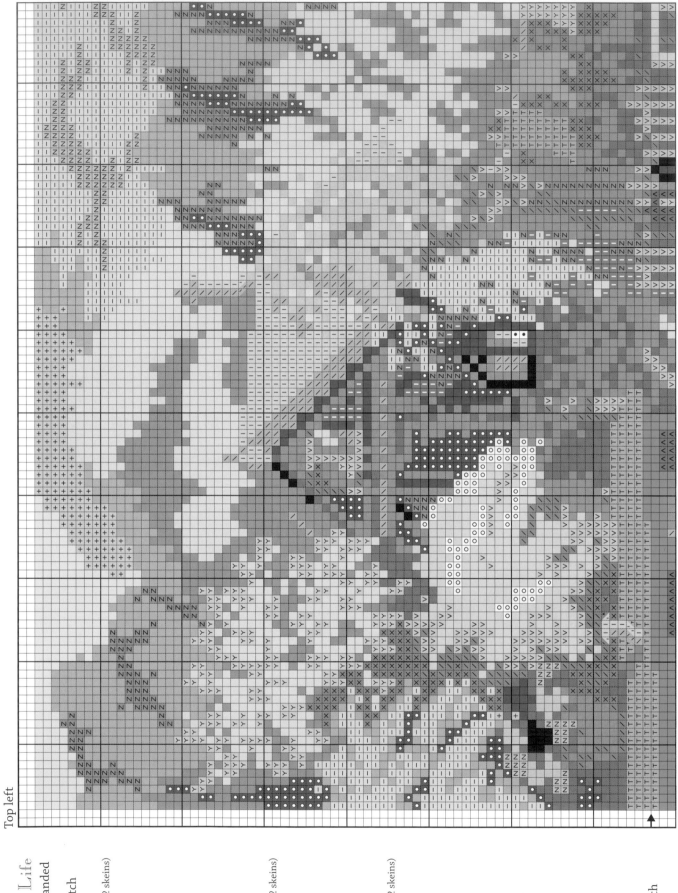

Top left

Canal Life

DMC stranded
cotton
Cross stitch

		168
/	169 (2 skeins)
	316
	334
Y	341
	347
	351
•	500
N	501
	502
X	520
	523 (2 skeins)
	535
\	611
>	612
O	727
	778
<	798
	827 (2 skeins)
−	911
⊤	993
	3012
I	3013
	3047
	3363
	3781
	3799
+	3813
	3822
	3847
	3848
•	blanc

Backstitch
— 535

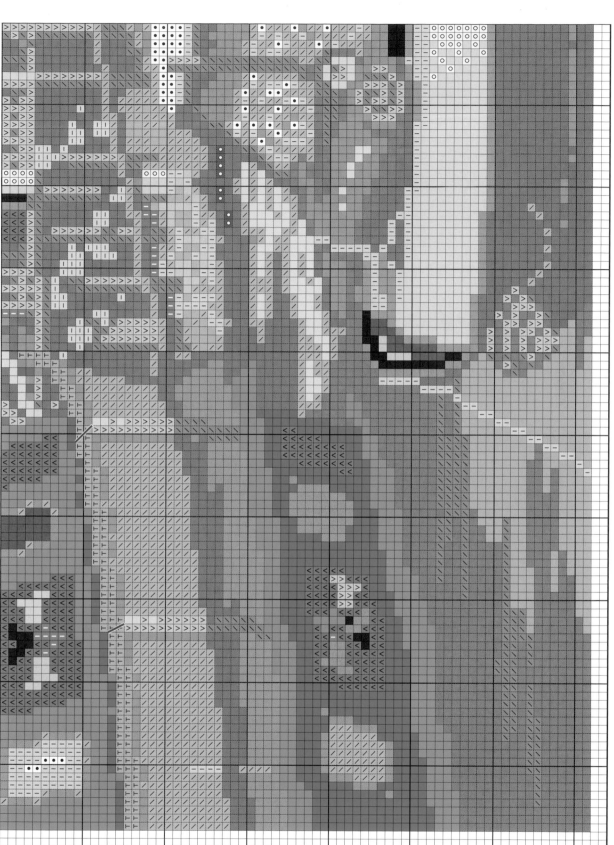

Top right

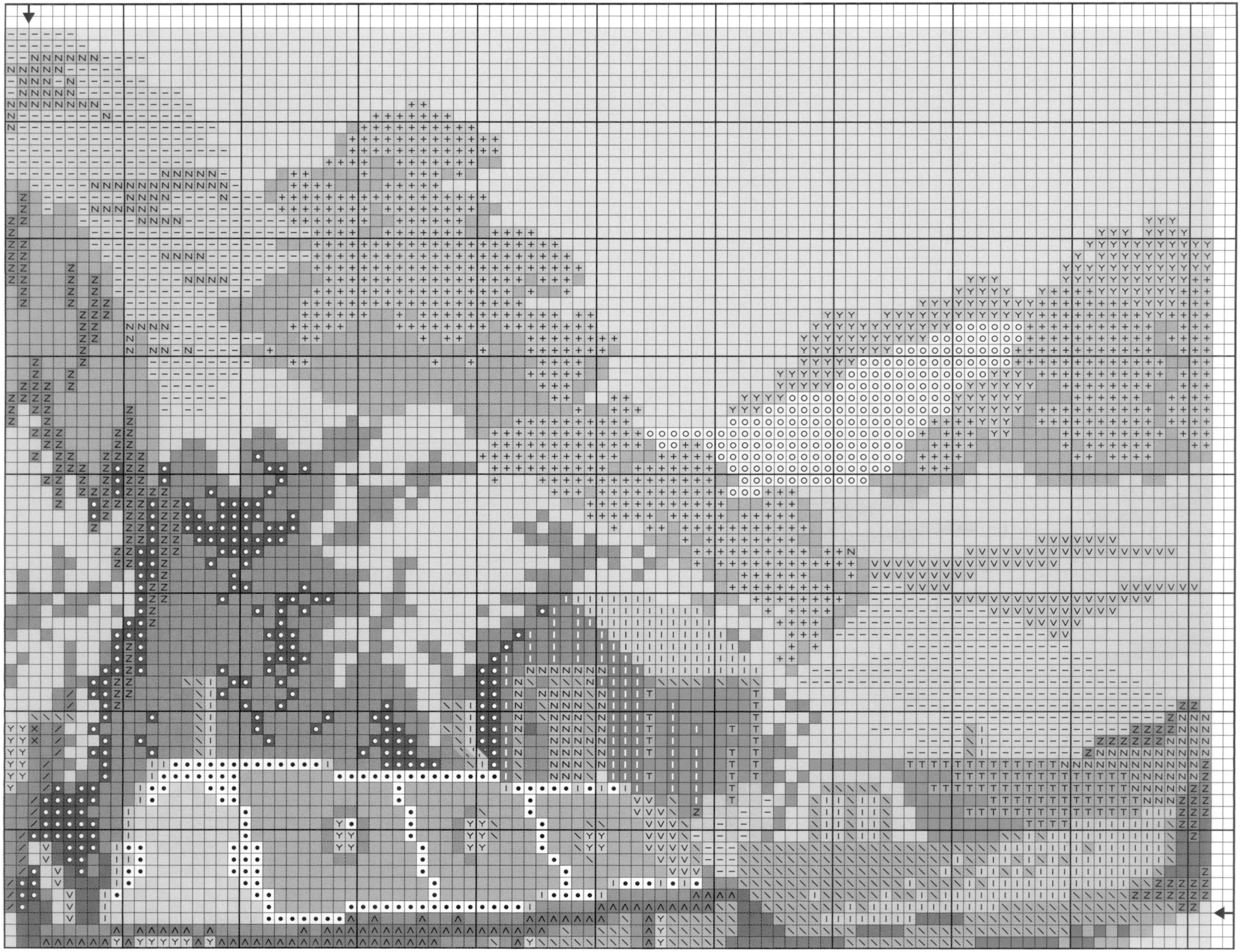

Canal Life

DMC stranded cotton
Cross stitch

Symbol	DMC
I	168
\	169 (2 skeins)
	316
	334
Y	341
	347
	351
•	500
Z	501
	502
X	520
	523 (2 skeins)
	535
/	611
V	612
O	727
	778
Λ	798
	827 (2 skeins)
I	911
T	993
N	3012
–	3013
	3047
	3363
	3781
	3799
+	3813
	3822
	3847
	3848
•	blanc

Backstitch
— 535

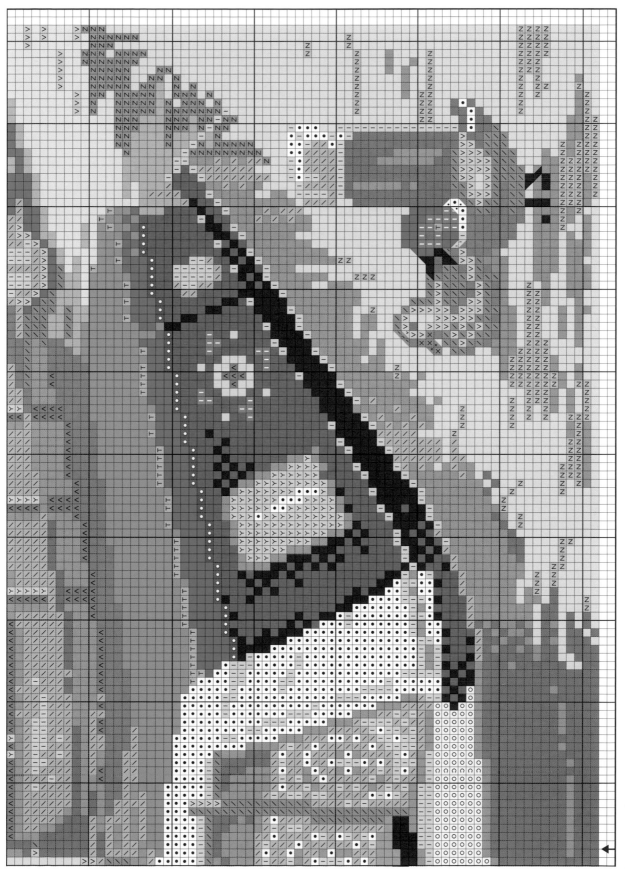

Designed by Claire Crompton

HARVEST TIME

*I*t's an early start at harvest time and dawn is just breaking but already the shire horses are being led across the fields to reap the crop, ready for the farmhands to gather the wheat into sheaves in the traditional way. Red poppies frame the scene, their colour echoed faintly in the distant sky.

In the past there was a strong community spirit, an understanding of the rhythm of the seasons and the need to work together and, literally, make hay while the sun shone. No wonder then that the whole village celebrated the safe gathering in of the harvest when it was so important, providing corn for the mill and fodder for the animals throughout the long, cold winter fast approaching.

Powerful draught horses were invaluable in the times before steam traction engines, before diesel power and modern combine harvesters. We may not see heavy horses at harvest time any more but in the rural counties of England watching the harvest being gathered in is still a deeply satisfying sight, as the combine cuts a swathe through the wheat and barley, leaving the fields neatly shorn and golden.

"WHEN THE SWALLOW'S NEST
IS HIGH, SUMMER IS DRY.
WHEN THE SWALLOW'S NEST IS
LOW, YOU CAN SAFELY
REAP AND SOW."

What an evocative scene this is – you can almost feel the warm sun on your back, hear the clink of the horses' harness and smell the freshly cut wheat. . . It makes a wonderful picture but would also be great as a firesceen.

GATHERING THE HARVEST PICTURE

This atmospheric scene would look fabulous made up as a wall hanging, framed with a country-print fabric to increase its size further. Alternatively, you could just stitch the lower two-thirds of the picture, to focus on the wonderful horses.

1 Prepare your fabric for work (see page 96). Find and mark the centre of the fabric and the centre of the chart on pages 82–85. For your own use you could photocopy the chart parts and tape them together. Mount your fabric in an embroidery frame if you wish.

2 Start stitching from the centre of the chart working outwards over one block of Aida (or two threads of linen). Use two strands of stranded cotton for full cross stitch and the areas of half cross stitch. Use one strand for backstitch. The backstitches are in a 'sketchy' style, which doesn't always follow the cross stitch exactly.

3 Once all the stitching is complete, frame as a picture (see page 100) or make up in another way of your choice.

Harvest Biscuits

Traditionally, harvest time was the busiest time of the year, often involving whole villages. A mid-morning snack would be welcomed by all.

❖ Heat the oven to 180°C (160° Fan/325°F/Gas Mark 4).
❖ In a food processor put 140g (5oz) of oats, 80g (3oz) caster sugar, 140g (5oz) soft butter, 50g (2oz) plain flour, 50g (2oz) chopped prunes (or dried apricots) and ½ teaspoon of mixed spice. Blend together in the processor (or in a bowl with a wooden spoon), until the dough clumps together.
❖ On a floured surface roll out the dough to about 6mm (¼in) thick, cut into circles or squares and put on a non-stick baking tray and bake for about 12 minutes.
❖ Cool on a wire rack and put the kettle on for a cup of tea.

'Tickle the earth with a hoe

and it will laugh a harvest.'

(Ralph Waldo Emerson)

HARVEST GIFTS

These three projects are a celebration of harvest time and early autumn and would be ideal to give as gifts at Harvest Festival. The sweet little harvest mouse design would also make a lovely greetings card or a little framed picture.

CORNUCOPIA CARD

STITCH COUNT
51h x 52w
DESIGN SIZE
9.5 x 9.5cm (3¾ x 3¾in)

This design with its overflowing horn of plenty would be perfect for a harvest time card or an autumn birthday. Stitch the motif opposite on a 15.2cm (6in) square of white 14-count Aida using two strands of stranded cotton for cross stitch and one for backstitch. Mount into a double-fold card with 10cm (4in) aperture – see page 101.

HARVEST MOUSE COASTER

STITCH COUNT
34h x 33w
DESIGN SIZE
6.2 x 6.2cm (2½ x 2½in)

A sweet little mouse on an ear of corn is small enough to decorate a coaster. The design could also become a card or gift tag. Stitch the motif on a 10.2cm (4in) square of white 14-count Aida using two strands of stranded cotton for cross stitch and one for backstitch. Back the embroidery with iron-on interfacing and trim to fit a square coaster with a 7.6cm (3in) aperture (see Suppliers).

SHEAVES TRINKET POT

STITCH COUNT
45h x 48w
DESIGN SIZE
7 x 7.6cm (2¾ x 3in)

This attractive design has been used in a trinket pot but could also become a card. Stitch the motif on a 12.7cm (5in) square of white 16-count Aida using two strands of stranded cotton for cross stitch and one for backstitch. Back the embroidery with iron-on interfacing and trim to fit into a wooden or ceramic trinket pot with a 9cm (3½in) diameter aperture (see Suppliers).

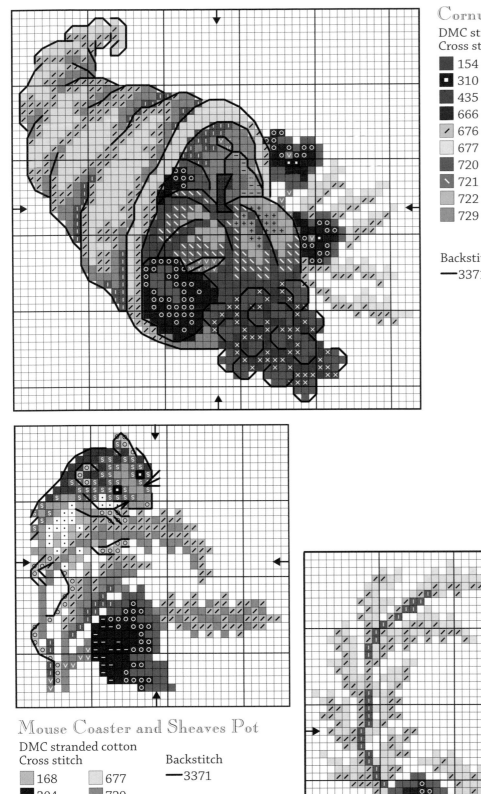

Cornucopia Card

DMC stranded cotton
Cross stitch

■	154	■	733
▣	310	−	734
■	435	V	3347
■	666	O	3705
/	676	■	3706
▨	677	I	3829
■	720	X	3834
\	721	■	3835
■	722	+	3854
■	729		

Backstitch
— 3371

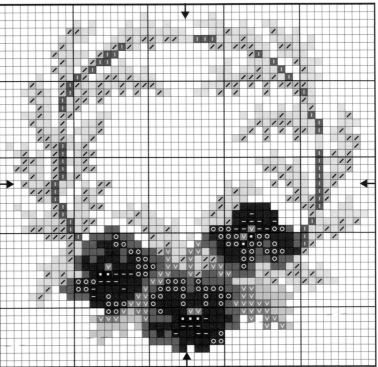

Mouse Coaster and Sheaves Pot

DMC stranded cotton
Cross stitch

■	168	▨	677
−	304	■	729
▣	310	V	3347
O	353	■	3348
■	435	O	3705
S	436	■	3706
■	437	I	3829
■	666	•	blanc
/	676		

Backstitch
— 3371

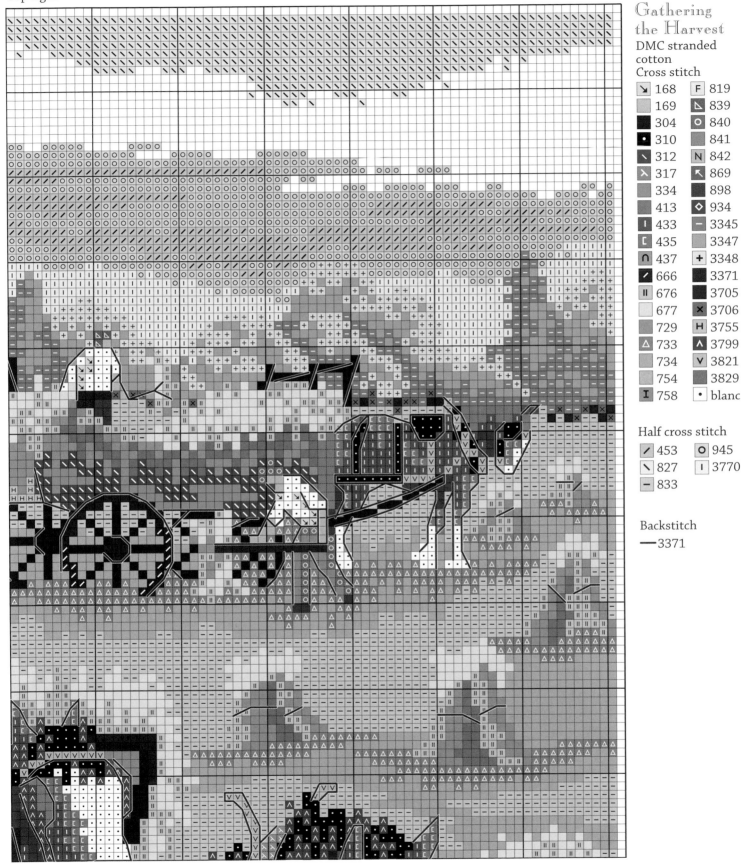

Gathering
the Harvest
DMC stranded
cotton
Cross stitch

↘	168	F	819
	169	◣	839
	304	⊙	840
⊡	310		841
↘	312	N	842
⋊	317	K	869
	334		898
	413	◇	934
I	433	−	3345
⊏	435		3347
∩	437	+	3348
⁄	666		3371
‖	676		3705
	677	✕	3706
	729	H	3755
△	733	∧	3799
	734	V	3821
	754		3829
I	758	•	blanc

Half cross stitch

⁄	453	O	945
↘	827	I	3770
−	833		

Backstitch
——3371

Bottom left

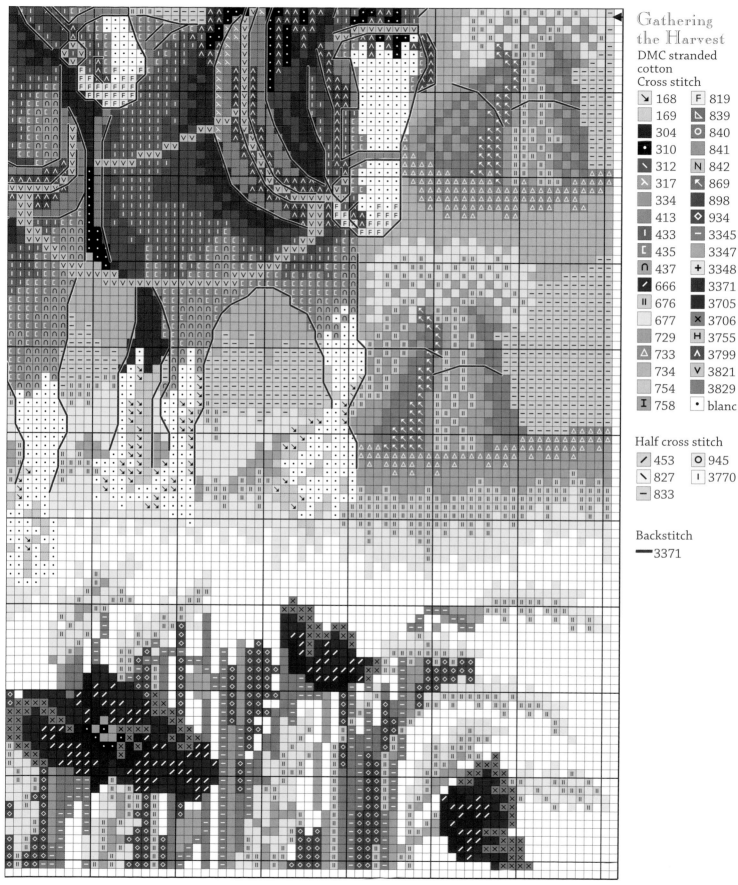

DMC stranded
cotton

Cross stitch

↘	168	F	819
	169	◣	839
	304	○	840
⊡	310		841
↘	312	N	842
⋋	317	K	869
	334		898
	413	◇	934
I	433	−	3345
C	435		3347
∩	437	+	3348
⁄	666		3371
‖	676		3705
	677	×	3706
	729	H	3755
△	733	∧	3799
	734	v	3821
	754		3829
I	758	•	blanc

Half cross stitch

⁄	453	○	945
↘	827	I	3770
−	833		

Backstitch

—3371

Bottom right

Designed by Lesley Teare

FIRST SNOWFALL

This traditional winter scene depicts the excitement that greets the first heavy snowfall of winter. Lights shine from the houses and church while the children have fun playing in the snow. Twilight is fading but they have waited all day with barely suppressed excitement until the madly swirling flakes of snow have accumulated into deep, pristine drifts. They are rewarded by a glistening white winter wonderland, perfect for snowball fights, tobogganing, ice skating and building huge snowmen. Ignoring cold fingers and toes, they will play for hours.

A robin, one of the most dearly loved birds, watches the fun, bringing a bright splash of colour to the scene. Holly and ivy also bring vivid colour, just as these evergreen plants themselves do throughout the depths of winter. In times past, holly was thought to bring fortune and fertility to a household, but only if brought into the house by a male member of the family. Ivy was long regarded as an emblem of fidelity and was often presented to newly wed couples.

A thick blanket of newly laid snow, with flakes still falling silently, will never lose its magic and the traditional winter scene portrayed by this lovely picture is still a common sight, especially in chillier northern climes.

"THE SQUEAK OF THE SNOW WILL THE TEMPERATURE SHOW."

This delightful design makes a lovely seasonal picture. The borders echo the pastoral view of winter and there are many small motifs that could be stitched individually.

SNOWFALL PICTURE

This cosy wintry scene could be made up as a lovely cushion for Christmas time. You could also stitch the borders for pretty bookmarks or use smaller motifs from the design to make cards and gift tags.

STITCH COUNT
168h x 196w

DESIGN SIZE
30.5 x 35.5cm (12 x 14in)

YOU WILL NEED
- 46 x 51cm (18 x 20in) mid blue 14-count Aida (Zweigart code 5130)
- Tapestry needle size 24
- DMC stranded cotton (floss) as listed in the chart key
- Kreinik #4 Very Fine Braid 101 platinum
- Suitable picture frame

'The first fall of snow is not only an event, it is a magical event. You go to bed in one kind of world and wake up to find yourself in another quite different, and if this is not enchantment, then where is it to be found?'

(J.B. Priestley)

1 Prepare your fabric for work (see page 96). Find and mark the centre of the fabric and the centre of the chart on pages 92–95. For your own use you could photocopy the chart parts and tape them together. Note: some colours use more than one skein – see the chart key for details. Mount your fabric in an embroidery frame if you wish.

2 Start stitching from the centre of the chart working outwards over one block of Aida. Use two strands of stranded cotton for full and three-quarter cross stitches and one strand of Kreinik thread. Use one strand for backstitches. The backstitches use a 'sketchy' style, which doesn't always follow the cross stitch exactly.

3 Once all the stitching is complete, frame the design as a picture (see page 100) or make up in another way of your choice.

Mulled Wine

A warming drink is perfect for icy-cold winter days and mulled wine is sure to bring colour to your cheeks.

- Pour a bottle of red wine into a saucepan and heat. Add a slug of brandy or rum and the juice of an orange.
- Add the zest of an orange and a lemon, some cinnamon sticks, a few cloves and some freshly grated nutmeg.
- Allow the wine to infuse for a few hours before serving hot.

"IF THE NORTH WIND
DOTH BLOW, THEN WE
SHALL HAVE SNOW."

WINTER WONDERS

These small projects are perfect for Christmas gifts. Stitch the cottage in the snow with sparkling stars as a seasonal card. The holly motif is perfect for a gift tag, while the snowflake motif makes a pretty decoration for a present.

FESTIVE CARD

STITCH COUNT
40h x 30w
DESIGN SIZE
7 x 5.5cm (2¾ x 2¼in)

This charming little design is very quick to stitch and embellish. Stitch the design charted opposite on to a piece of 14-count pale blue Aida 12.7 x 10.2cm (5 x 4in), using two strands for cross stitch and one strand for the Kreinik metallic thread. Mount into a double-fold card and embellish as desired.

HOLLY TAG

STITCH COUNT
18h x 29w
DESIGN SIZE
3.2 x 5cm (1¼ x 2in)

This holly motif could also be stitched repeatedly on Aida band to make a cake band. Stitch on to 14-count pale blue Aida 7.6 x 10.2cm (3 x 4in), using two strands for cross stitch and one for backstitch. Use one strand of Kreinik thread. Trim to 6.3 x 9cm (2½ x 3½in) and fray the edges. Cut a piece of red card, punch a hole in the corner for a ribbon loop. Glue the embroidery to the card.

PRESENT DECORATION

STITCH COUNT
24h x 24w
DESIGN SIZE
4.5 x 4.5 (1¾ x 1¾in)

Add a special finishing touch to a Christmas gift with this sparkly decoration. Stitch the design on to a 7.6cm (3in) square of 14-count perforated silver paper. Trim the paper to within one row of the stitches. Fix the decoration to a present with double-side tape and add a ribbon loop on the back. Add sequin embellishments as desired. The decoration could also be used as a tree ornament.

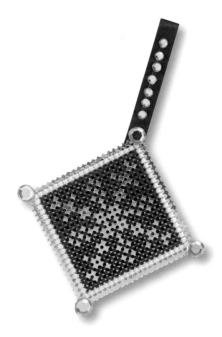

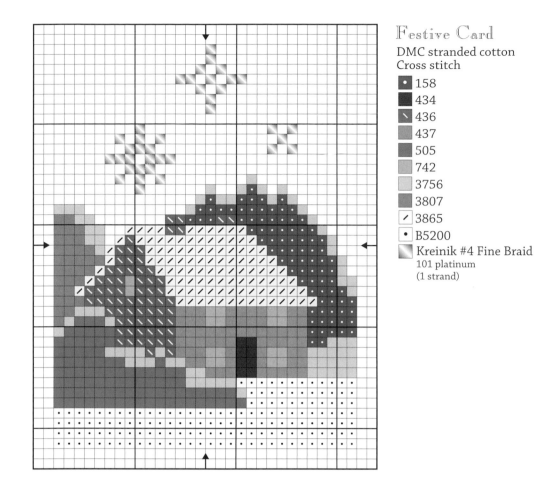

Festive Card

DMC stranded cotton
Cross stitch

- ● 158
- ■ 434
- ◨ 436
- ▦ 437
- ▦ 505
- ▦ 742
- ▦ 3756
- ▦ 3807
- ◹ 3865
- • B5200
- ◪ Kreinik #4 Fine Braid
  101 platinum
  (1 strand)

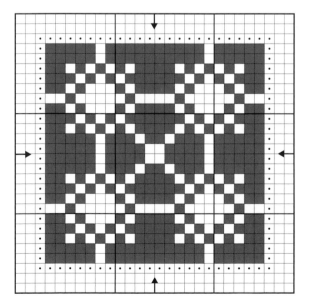

Present Decoration

DMC stranded cotton
Cross stitch

- ■ 158
- • B5200

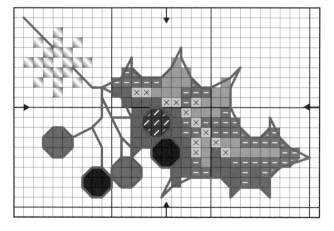

Holly Tag

DMC stranded cotton
Cross stitch

			Backstitch
✖ 164	▦ 351	▬ 905	▬ 839
■ 347	▦ 703	◪ Kreinik #4	
◹ 349	▦ 904	Fine Braid	
		101 platinum	
		(1 strand)	

Snowfall
Picture

DMC stranded cotton
Cross stitch

·	156			
	(2 skeins)			
I	158			
/	159			
+	164			
×	169			
·	310			
I	319			
N	922			
U	347			
V	349			
−	928			
	950			
✓	3747			
	435			
	(2 skeins)			
I	3807			
O	436			
	437			
	505			
	561			
	562			
	(2 skeins)			
·	B5200			
	(3 skeins)			
/	Kreinik #4			
	101 platinum			
	(1 strand)			
	(3 reels)			

·	745
I	794
/	839
	(2 skeins)
+	904
	905
	921
	927
	351
/	434
I	3756
	3854
	3862
	3865
✓	703
s	742

Backstitch
———— 839
———— B5200

French knots
● 310

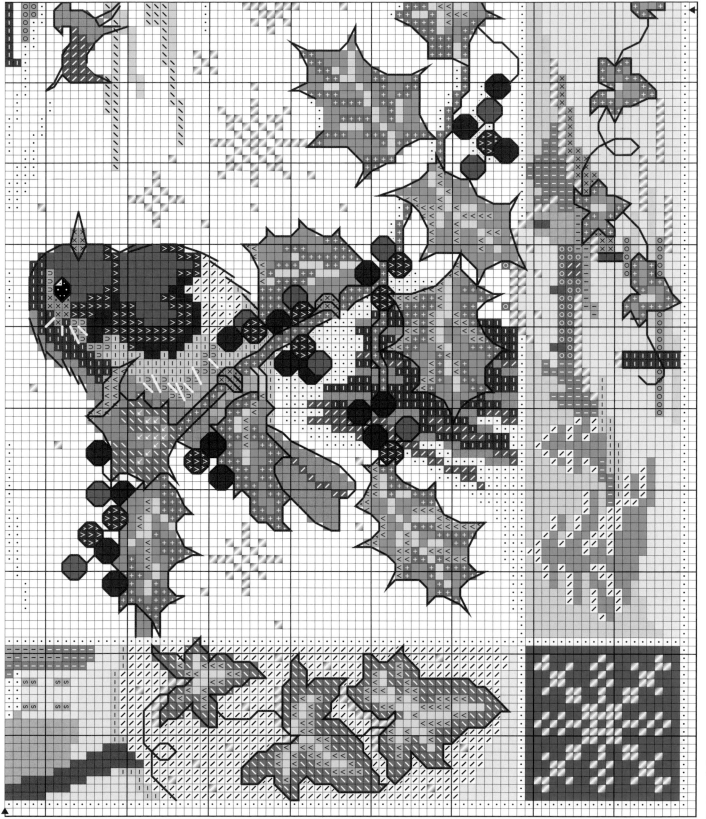

Snowfall Picture

DMC stranded cotton
Cross stitch

156 (2 skeins)		
158	−	794
O	159	839 (2 skeins)
+	164	904
×	169	905
·	310	921
I	319	922
N	347	927
U	349	928
−	351	950
/	434	3747
		435	3756 (2 skeins)
O	436	3807
I	437	3854
/	505	3862
	561	3865
K	562	B5200 (3 skeins)
⋀	703	Kreinik #4 101 platinum (1 strand) (3 reels)
S	742	

Backstitch
——— 839
———— B5200

French knots
● 310

Top right

— 94 —

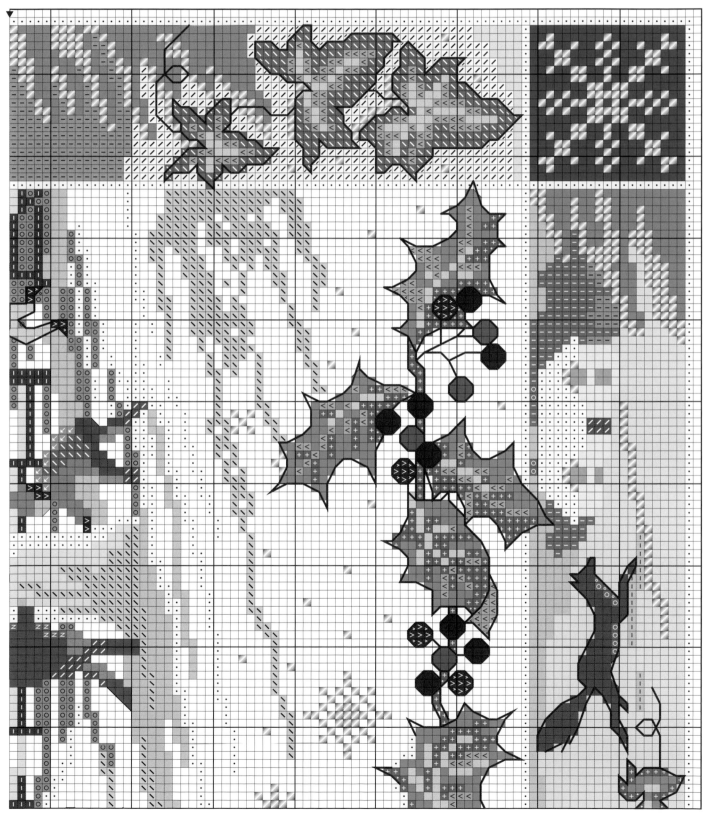

MATERIALS AND TECHNIQUES

This section will be useful to beginners as it describes the materials and equipment required and the basic techniques and stitches needed to work the projects. Framing pictures and mounting work in cards is described on pages 100 and 101. Refer to Suppliers for useful addresses.

MATERIALS

Very few materials are required for cross stitch embroidery, although some of the projects in this book have been given an additional sparkle and texture by the use of seed beads

FABRICS

The designs have been worked predominantly on a blockweave fabric called Aida. If you change the gauge (count) of the material, that is the number of holes per inch, then the size of the finished work will alter accordingly. Some of the designs have been stitched on linen and in this case need to be worked over two fabric threads instead of one block.

THREADS

The projects have been stitched with DMC stranded embroidery cotton (floss) but you could match the colours to other thread ranges – ask at your local needlework store. The six-stranded skeins can easily be split into separate threads. The project instructions tell you how many strands to use. Some of the larger designs use more than one skein of thread – refer to the chart keys.

NEEDLES

Tapestry needles, available in different sizes, are used for cross stitch as they have a rounded point and do not snag fabric.

SCISSORS

You will need two pairs of scissors: a pair of dressmaking shears for cutting fabrics and a small pair of sharp-pointed embroidery scissors for cutting and trimming threads.

FRAMES

It is a matter of personal preference as to whether you use an embroidery frame or hoop to keep your fabric taut while stitching. Generally speaking, working with a frame helps to keep the tension even and prevent distortion, while working without a frame is faster and less cumbersome. There are various types on the market – look in your local needlework or craft store.

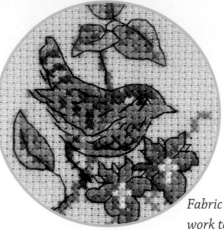

Fabric and threads should work together to create a harmonious image

TECHNIQUES

Cross stitch embroidery requires few complicated techniques but your stitching will look its best if you follow the simple guidelines below.

PREPARING THE FABRIC

Spending a little time preparing your embroidery fabric before stitching will save time and trouble in the long run.

⬧ Before starting work, check the design size given with each project and make sure that this is the size you require for your finished embroidery. Your fabric must be larger than the finished design size to allow for making up, so allow 13cm (5in) to both dimensions when stitching a sampler and 7.5cm (3in) for smaller projects.

⬧ Before beginning to stitch, neaten the fabric edges either by hemming or zigzagging to prevent fraying as you work. If using plastic canvas, neaten all the edges by trimming off any sharp or rough pieces.

⬧ Find the centre of the fabric. This is important regardless of which direction you work from, in order to stitch the design centrally on the fabric. To find the centre, fold the fabric in half horizontally and then vertically, then tack (baste) along the folds (or use tailor's chalk). The centre point is where the two lines of tacking meet. This point on the fabric should correspond to the centre point on the chart. Remove these lines on completion of the work.

Calculating Design Size

Each project gives the stitch count and finished design size but if you want to work the design on a different count fabric you will need to re-calculate the finished size. Divide the numbers of stitches in the design by the fabric count number, e.g., 140 x 140 ÷ 14-count = a design size of 10 x 10in (25.5 x 25.5cm). Working on evenweave or linen usually means working over two threads, so divide the fabric count by two before you start calculating.

Using Charts and Keys

The charts in this book are easy to work from. Each square on the chart represents one stitch. Each coloured square, or coloured square with a symbol, represents a thread colour, with the code number given in the chart key. A few of the designs use fractional stitches (three-quarter cross stitches) to give more definition to the design. Solid coloured lines show where backstitches or long stitches are to be worked. French knots are shown by coloured circles.

Each complete chart has arrows at the sides to show the centre point (see example below), which you could mark with a pen. Where the charts have been split over several pages, the key is repeated. For your own use, you could colour photocopy and enlarge charts, taping the parts together.

Starting and Finishing Stitching

It is always a good idea to start and finish work correctly, to create the neatest effect and avoid ugly bumps and threads trailing across the back of work. To finish off thread, pass the needle through several nearby stitches on the wrong side of the work, then cut the thread off, close to the fabric.

Knotless Loop Start

Starting this way can be very useful with stranded cotton (floss), but only works if you are intending to stitch with an even number of threads, i.e. 2, 4, or 6. Cut the stranded cotton roughly twice the length you would normally need and separate one strand. Double this strand and thread your needle with the two ends. Pierce your fabric from the wrong side where you intend to place your first stitch, leaving the looped end at the back of the work. Return your needle to the wrong side after forming a half cross stitch and pass the needle through the waiting loop. You can now begin to stitch.

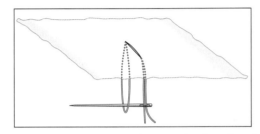

Fig 1 Beginning stitching with a knotless loop

Away Waste Knot Start

Start this way if working with an odd number of strands or when using variegated threads. Thread your needle and make a knot at the end. Take the needle and thread through from the front of the fabric to the back and come up again about 2.5cm (1in) away from the knot. Now either start cross stitching and work towards the knot, cutting it off when the threads are anchored, or thread the end into your needle and finish off under some completed stitches.

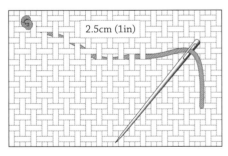

Fig 2 Beginning stitching with an away waste knot

Washing and Pressing

If you need to wash your finished embroidery, first make sure the stranded cottons are colourfast by washing them in tepid water and mild soap. Rinse well and lay out flat to dry completely before stitching. Wash completed embroideries in the same way. Iron on a medium setting, covering the ironing board with a thick layer of towels. Place stitching right side down on the towels and press gently.

Stitch Basics

The stitches used for the projects in this book are all extremely easy to work – follow the instructions and diagrams here.

Backstitch

Backstitches are used to give definition to parts of a design and to outline areas. Many of the charts used different coloured backstitches.

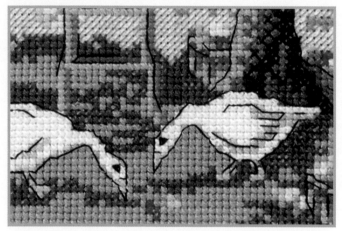

Many designs use a 'sketchy' backstitch style, which doesn't always outline the cross stitches exactly

To work backstitch follow the diagram below, bringing the needle up at 1 and down at 2. Then bring the needle up again at 3 and down at 4, and so on.

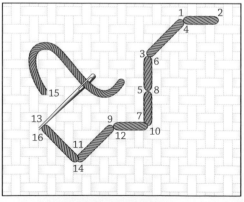

Fig 3 The sequence for working backstitch

Blanket Stitch

Blanket stitch is worked in a similar way to buttonhole stitch and has been used to edge the placemat, napkin holder and cutlery case in the Summer Skies chapter.

Begin with a knotted thread, with the knot hidden inside the project and bring the thread out at the edge of the project where you wish to start. Make a stitch about 6mm (¼in) long (see diagram below) and then bring the needle out about 6mm (¼in) further along, with the working thread under the needle so a loop is formed. Continue all along the edge all round and fasten off invisibly.

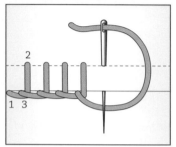

Fig 4 Working blanket stitch

Cross Stitch

A cross stitch can be worked singly over one block of Aida (Fig 5a) or over two threads of linen or evenweave fabric (Fig 5b).

To make a cross stitch on Aida, bring the needle up through the fabric at the bottom right side of the stitch (number 1 on Fig 5a) and cross diagonally to number 2. Push the needle through the hole and bring up at 3, crossing diagonally to 4. To work the next stitch, come up through the bottom left corner of the first stitch and repeat the sequence above.

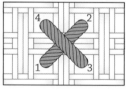 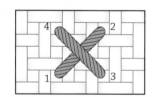

Fig 5a Working a single cross stitch on Aida fabric   *Fig 5b Working a single cross stitch on evenweave fabric*

A design doesn't always require backstitch: pure cross stitch can create some beautiful scenes

FRENCH KNOT

French knots have been used as highlights and details in some of the designs, in various colours. To work, follow the diagrams below, bringing the needle and thread up through the fabric at the exact place where the knot is to be positioned. Wrap the thread once or twice around the needle (according to the project instructions), holding the thread firmly close to the needle, then twist the needle back through the fabric as close as possible to where it first emerged. Holding the knot down carefully, pull the thread through to the back leaving the knot on the surface, securing it with one small stitch on the back.

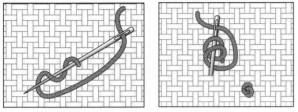

Fig 6 Working a French knot

French knots provide useful accents and texture to a design. You could use seed beads instead

LONG STITCH

You may use this stitch occasionally, for example for flower stamens or butterfly antennae, or if working back-stitch in a freer style. Simply work a long, straight stitch starting and finishing at the points indicated on the chart.

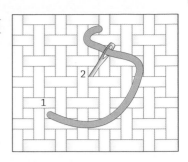

Fig 7 Working a long stitch

THREE-QUARTER CROSS STITCH

Three-quarter cross stitches give more detail to a design and can create the illusion of curves. They are shown by a triangle within a square on the charts. Working three-quarter cross stitches is easier on evenweave fabric than Aida (see diagram below). To work on Aida, work a half cross stitch across the diagonal and then anchor this with a quarter stitch from the corner into the centre of the Aida square, piercing the fabric.

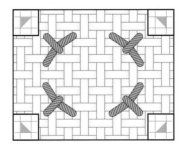

Fig 8 Working three-quarter cross stitch on evenweave

Tips for Perfect Stitching

Counted cross stitch is one of the easiest forms of counted embroidery. Following these useful tips will help you to produce neat work.

❖ Check the design size given with each project and make sure that this is the size you require for your finished embroidery. Your fabric should be at least 5cm (2in) larger all round than the finished size of the stitching, to allow for making up.

❖ Organize your threads before you start a project to avoid confusion later. Put the threads required for a particular project on an organizer (available from craft shops) and always include the manufacturer's name and the shade number. You can make your own thread organizer by punch holes along one side of a piece of thick card.

❖ When you have cut the length of stranded cotton (floss) you need, usually about 46cm (18in), separate out all the strands before taking the number you need, realigning them and threading your needle.

❖ If using a hoop, avoid placing it over worked stitches and remove it from fabric at the end of a stitching session.

❖ For neat cross stitching, work the top stitches so they all face in the same direction.

❖ If your thread begins to twist, turn the work upside down and let the needle spin.

❖ If adding a backstitch outline, add it after the completed cross stitch to prevent the backstitch line being broken.

Making Up

Making up the projects is described in the relevant chapters but two frequently used methods are described here – mounting and framing a picture and mounting work in cards.

Mounting and Framing

It really is best to take large cross stitch samplers and pictures to a professional framer, where you can choose from a wide variety of mounts and frames that will best enhance your work. The framer will be able to stretch the fabric correctly and cut mounts accurately. You can also select more unusual mounts, such as ovals. If you intend to mount the work yourself, use acid-free mounting board in a colour that will not show through the embroidery and follow the method described below.

1 Cut a piece of mount board to fit the frame aperture (draw around the frame's backing board). Using double-sided tape, stick a piece of wadding (batting) to the mount board and trim the wadding to the same size using a sharp craft knife.

2 Lay the embroidery right side up on to the wadding, making sure the design is central and straight by matching a fabric thread along the edges. Push pins through at the four corners and along the edges to mark the position. Trim the fabric to leave about 5cm (2in) all around.

3 Turn the embroidery and mount board over together and stick double-sided tape around the edges of the board to a depth of 5cm (2in). Peel the backing off the tape. Fold the excess fabric back, pressing down firmly to stick the fabric to the board, adding more tape to neaten the corners. Remove the pins and reassemble the frame with the embroidery in it. It is not necessary to use the glass; in fact this can often spoil the work as it flattens the stitches when they are pushed against it.

MOUNTING WORK INTO CARDS

Many of the designs or parts of larger designs can be stitched and made up into cards and there are many styles of card mounts available today. Some are simple single-fold cards, while others are pre-folded with three sections, the middle one having a window or aperture for your embroidery.

MOUNTING WORK ON A SINGLE-FOLD CARD

1 Trim your embroidery to the size required leaving two or three extra rows all round if you want a fringe around the stitching.

2 Pull away the outer fabric threads to form the fringe and use then double-sided tape to attach the embroidery to the front of your card.

MOUNTING WORK IN A DOUBLE-FOLD CARD

1 Position the embroidery in the card's window space – the fabric should be at least 2.5cm (1in) larger than the aperture all round, so trim it if necessary.

2 Place strips of double-sided adhesive tape on the card to fix the embroidery (some cards already have this).

3 Peel the backing from the tape and fold over the third of the card to cover. This can also be secured with tape for a neater finish. For a personal touch add ribbons, bows, buttons, charms and so on to finish.

MAKING A DOUBLE-FOLD CARD

You can make your own double-fold cards, which will allow you to match a card colour to your embroidery. The instructions below are for a small card but you can change the dimensions to suit your embroidery by working with a larger piece of cardstock. Choose card thick enough to support your stitching – between 160–240gsm. You will need: thick cardstock in a colour of your choice; cutting mat; craft knife; metal ruler; embossing tool and bone folder (optional).

1 Choose a card colour to complement your embroidery and cut a piece 30 x 12.7cm (12 x 5in) as shown in Fig 9 (or to the size of your choice). On the wrong side of the card, use a pencil to draw two lines dividing the card into three sections of 10cm (4in). Score gently along each line with the back of a craft knife or an embossing tool to make folding easier. Do not cut through the card.

2 In the centre section, mark an aperture slightly bigger than the finished size of the design with a pencil, leaving a border of about 2.5cm (1in) at the top and bottom and about 1.3cm (½in) at the sides (or the size of your choice). Place the card on a cutting mat and cut out the aperture with a sharp craft knife and metal ruler, carefully cutting into the corners neatly.

3 Trim the left edge of the first section by 2mm (⅛in) so that it lies flat when folded over to the inside of the card. This will cover the back of the stitching. Fold the left and then the right section on the scored lines – a bone folder will help you to create a nice, sharp fold. The card is now ready for you to mount your embroidery.

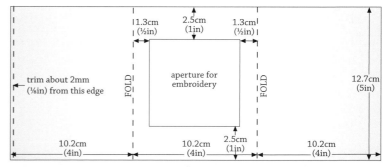

Fig 9 Making a double-fold card

THE DESIGNERS

CLAIRE CROMPTON

Claire studied knitwear design at college before joining the design team at DMC, and finally going freelance. Claire's work has appeared in several magazines, including *Cross Stitch Magic*. Her designs also feature in six David & Charles books: *Cross Stitch Greetings Cards*, *Cross Stitch Alphabets*, *Cross Stitch Angels*, *Cross Stitch Fairies*, *Magical Cross Stitch* and *Quick to Stitch Cross Stitch Cards*, and in her solo books *Cross Stitch Card Collection*, *Picture Your Pet in Cross Stitch* and *Christmas Cross Stitch*, also published by David & Charles. Claire lives in Gunnislake, Cornwall.

CAROLINE PALMER

Originally attracted to painting and illustration, Caroline went on to qualify in Textile Design before becoming interested in embroidery. In 1992, following a distinction in the City & Guilds embroidery course, she was selected by the Embroiderer's Guild to receive a complementary stand to display her mixed technique embroidery work at the annual Knitting & Stitching show at Alexandra Palace. Now specializing in cross stitch, Caroline designs regularly for cross stitch magazines and her work has also appeared in several craft books, including *Cross Stitch Alphabets* for David & Charles. Her designs for this book were inspired by her surroundings since moving from London to the West Country.

LESLEY TEARE

Lesley trained as a textile designer, with a degree in printed and woven textiles. For some years she has been one of DMC's leading designers and her designs have also featured in many of the cross stitch magazines. Lesley has contributed to five other books for David & Charles – *Cross Stitch Greetings Cards*, *Cross Stitch Alphabets*, *Cross Stitch Angels*, *Cross Stitch Fairies* and *Magical Cross Stitch*. She has also authored four solo books for David & Charles – *101 Weekend Cross Stitch Gifts*, *Travel the World in Cross Stitch*, *Oriental Cross Stitch* and *Fantasy Cross Stitch*. Lesley lives in Hitcham, Suffolk.

CAROL THORNTON

Carol began her career in Arts and Crafts as a photographic artist using airbrush. Subsequently she was part of the design teams of Crossley Carpets and Firths Carpets, and later moved into screen printing. She has a combined degree in Textile Design and Science and is a freelance designer of printed and stitched textiles, working with many companies including John Wilmans, Harlequin and Crown in print, and DMC, Coats Craft and The Craft Collection in stitching. Her paintings are published as fine art prints, and she also converts them for stitching magazines such as *Stitch with the Embroiderers Guild*, *Cross Stitch Gold* and *World of Cross Stitching*. Her designs previously featured in *Magical Cross Stitch*, also published by David & Charles.

SUPPLIERS

UK

Coats Crafts UK
PO Box 22, Lingfield House,
McMullen Road, Darlington,
County Durham DL1 1YQ
Tel: 01325 394237 (helpline)
www.coatscrafts.co.uk
For Anchor stranded cotton (floss) and other embroidery supplies.

Creative Crafts & Needlework
18 High Street, Totnes, Devon TQ9 5RY
Tel: 01803 866002
www.creative-crafts-needlework.co.uk
For general needlework and craft supplies, including DMC and Anchor threads

Craft Creations Ltd
Ingersoll House, Delamare Road,
Cheshunt, Hertfordshire, EN8 9HD
Tel: 01992 781900
Email: enquiries@craftcreations.com
www.craftcreations.com
For card mounts and card-making accessories. The Woodland Greetings cards used cream double-fold cards with a circular aperture (code AP03U)

DMC Creative World Ltd
1st Floor Compass Building, Feldspar
Close, Enderby, Leicestershire LE19 4SD
Tel: 0116 275 4000
Fax: 0116 275 4000
www.dmccreative.co.uk
For embroidery fabrics, stranded cotton, metallic threads and other embroidery supplies

Framecraft Miniatures Ltd
Unit 3, Isis House, Lindon Road,
Brownhills, West Midlands WS8 7BW
Tel/Fax (UK): 01543 360842
Tel (international): 44 1543 453154
Email: sales@framecraft.com
www.framecraft.com
For wooden trinket bowls and boxes, notebook covers, pincushions, coasters and many other pre-finished items with cross stitch inserts, including the harvest mouse coaster and the sheaves trinket pot on page 80

Heritage Stitchcraft
Redbrook Lane, Brereton, Rugeley,
Staffordshire WS15 1QU
Tel: 01889 575256
Email: enquiries@heritagestitchcraft.com
www.heritagestitchcraft.com
For Zweigart fabrics and other embroidery supplies

Madeira Threads (UK) Ltd
PO Box 6, Thirsk, North Yorkshire
YO7 3YX
Tel: 01845 524880
Email: info@madeira.co.uk
www.madeira.co.uk
For Madeira stranded cottons and other embroidery supplies. To contact Madeira for a thread conversion chart ring 01765 640003

Brenda Walton
www.kandcompany.com
For the sculptured insect charms used on the Woodland Greetings cards on page 32

USA

Joann Stores, Inc
5555 Darrow Road, Hudson Ohio
Tel: 1 888 739 4120
Email: guest service@jo-annstores.com
www.joann.com
For general needlework and quilting supplies (mail order and shops across the US)

MCG Textiles
13845 Magnolia Avenue,
Chino, CA 91710
Tel: 909 591-6351
www.mcgtextiles.com
For cross stitch fabrics and pre-finished items

M & J Buttons
1000 Sixth Avenue,
New York, NY 10018
Tel: 212 391 6200
www.mjtrim.com
For beads, buttons, ribbons and trimmings

Mill Hill, a division of Wichelt Imports Inc.
N162 Hwy 35, Stoddard WI 54658
Tel: 608 788 4600
Email: millhill@millhill.com
www.millhill.com
For Mill Hill beads and Framecraft products

ACKNOWLEDGMENTS

The publishers would like to thank the following designers for their contributions: Claire Crompton, Caroline Palmer, Lesley Teare and Carol Thornton. In addition, we would like to express our thanks to Lin Clements who has done a superb job of managing the project, originating an entertaining and very readable text, and preparing excellent charts.

Lesley Teare would like to thank Tina Godwin for stitching the Country Cottage picture and the First Snowfall picture. Claire Crompton would like to thank DMC Creative World for generously supplying the threads used in her designs in this book. Carol Thornton would like to thank DMC and Cara Ackerman for supplying the materials for the stitching of her projects. Thanks also to Creative Crafts & Needlework for materials supplied for the Alfresco Collection.

INDEX